KEY FACTS

# INTELLECTUAL PROPERTY

JAMES GRIFFIN,
JANE YING AND
ABHILASH NAIR

Hodder Arnold
A MEMBER OF THE HODDER HEADLINE GROUP

Orders: please contact Bookpoint Ltd, 130 Milton Park, Abingdon, Oxon OX14 4SB. Telephone: (44) 01235 827720. Fax: (44) 01235 400454. Lines are open from 9.00–5.00, Monday to Saturday, with a 24 hour message answering service. You can also order through our website www.hoddereducation.co.uk

If you have any comments to make about this, or any of our other titles, please send them to educationenquiries@hodder.co.uk

*British Library Cataloguing in Publication Data*
A catalogue record for this title is available from the British Library

ISBN: 978 0 340 94027 3

This Edition Published 2007
Impression number 10 9 8 7 6 5 4 3 2 1
Year 2011 2010 2009 2008 2007



Typeset by Transet Limited, Coventry, England
Printed in Great Britain for Hodder Arnold, an imprint of Hodder Education, a member of the Hodder Headline Group, 338 Euston Road, London NW1 3BH by by Cox & Wyman Ltd, Reading, Berkshire.

# CONTENTS

# PREFACE

The Key Facts series is a practical and complete revision aid that can be used by students of law courses at all levels from A Level to degree and beyond, and in professional and vocational courses.

The Key Facts series is designed to give a clear view of each subject. This will be useful to students when tackling new topics and is invaluable as a revision aid. Most chapters open with an outline in diagram form of the points covered in that chapter. The points are then developed in a structured list form to make learning easier. Supporting cases are given throughout by name and, for some complex areas, facts are given to reinforce the point being made.

The Key Facts series aims to accommodate the syllabus content of most qualifications in a subject area, using many visual learning aids.

The law is stated as we believe it to be on 30th October 2006.

# CHAPTER 1

# INTRODUCTION

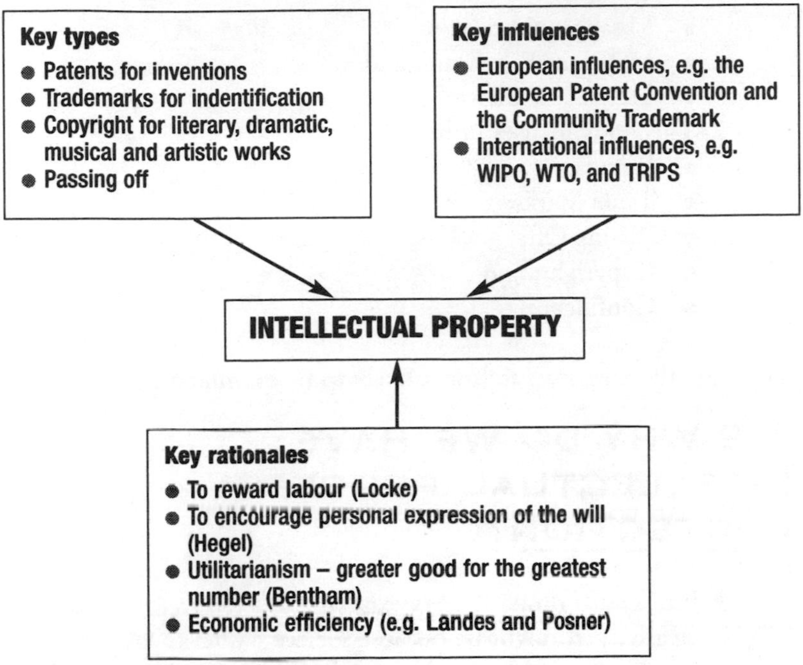

**Key types**
- Patents for inventions
- Trademarks for indentification
- Copyright for literary, dramatic, musical and artistic works
- Passing off

**Key influences**
- European influences, e.g. the European Patent Convention and the Community Trademark
- International influences, e.g. WIPO, WTO, and TRIPS

**INTELLECTUAL PROPERTY**

**Key rationales**
- To reward labour (Locke)
- To encourage personal expression of the will (Hegel)
- Utilitarianism – greater good for the greatest number (Bentham)
- Economic efficiency (e.g. Landes and Posner)

## 1.1 INTELLECTUAL PROPERTY

1. 'Intellectual Property' is a term of relatively recent origin, used as an umbrella term to cover many different types of 'rights'. These may include the following areas:
   - Copyrights;
   - Patents;
   - Trade Marks;
   - Passing Off;
   - Confidence;
   - Unfair Competition;

- Performance Rights;
- Trade Secrets;
- Registered Design Rights;
- Unregistered Design Rights;
- Contract;
- Misappropriation;
- Malicious Falsehood; and
- Trespass to Chattels.

2. This book focuses upon:
   - Patents;
   - Trade Marks;
   - Passing Off;
   - Copyright; and
   - Confidence.

These are the areas you are most likely to be examined upon.

## 1.2 WHY DO WE HAVE INTELLECTUAL PROPERTY PROTECTION?

1. Intellectual property may exist due to a desire to encourage creativity. It might be because society wishes to ensure reimbursement for the labour of individuals. Alternatively it could be to encourage economic efficiency. Ultimately, there is no hard and fast answer.
2. The work of philosopher John Locke, although not necessarily written with intellectual property protection in mind, refers to the need to reward labour. The precise delimitation of the notion of reward is uncertain. However, it may be said that it is to provide adequate reward, whatever that may be, up to the extent that there is 'enough and good' left for others, and that there is not 'waste'.
3. Georg Hegel was another philosopher who is often referred to within the context of intellectual property. He suggested that property is a way of expressing the will. The application

to intellectual property law is self-evident, in that this theory would suggest legal protection is given to protect the manifestation of the will.

4. Jeremy Bentham is used to justify intellectual property on utilitarian grounds. This is in accordance with the notion of balancing the interests of right-holders with the interests of recipients (or others receiving the item protected by the 'right').
5. There are economic arguments, such as those put forward by Merges and Nelson, and Landes and Posner. Merges and Nelson warn against over-protection, and Landes and Posner suggest an optimal level of protection. There is a famous debate between Merges and Nelson and Kitch. Kitch argued that broad prospecting patents would encourage creativity, whereas Merges and Nelson suggested they could stifle invention.

## 1.3 THE DIFFERENT TYPES OF INTELLECTUAL PROPERTY

1. The types of intellectual property mentioned in paragraph 1.1 are not mutually exclusive. An item may have a number of types of intellectual property embedded within it. A chocolate bar may have patents concerning its method of manufacture, copyright may protect the text printed on the packaging, and a trademark may also apply to the representation of the name. These and additional rights may also pertain to the shape of the packaging.
2. A patent is concerned with applied technology – namely how things work – not with abstract ideas.
3. The subject matter of a patent is an invention. An invention can be either a product (a tangible item), a process (a method of making something *or* a means of using something) or a product-by-process.
4. A patent is granted by the Patent Office for a maximum period of 20 years (calculated from the date of application)

and confers on the patentee an exclusive right to make, offer, dispose of, keep or use the product, or to use or offer the process which is the subject matter of the patent. The relevant legislation is the Patents Act 1977.

5. A trade mark is a sign or symbol used in the course of trade to indicate the commercial origin of goods or services.
   - Trade marks enable consumers to distinguish one product from another and to choose between competing brands.
   - A sign must be capable of graphic representation; capable of distinguishing the goods or services of one undertaking from those of another; and must not fall within the list of absolute grounds for refusal, nor must it fall within any of the relative grounds for refusal.
6. Once registered a trade mark is valid for ten years. However, it may be renewed indefinitely.
7. Registration does not mean that the mark is automatically safe from counter-attack; for instance, where the proprietor has failed to look after the mark, they may have made it vulnerable to an action for revocation by a third party.
8. Registration gives the proprietor the exclusive right to prevent others from using the same or similar sign in the course of trade in relation to the same or similar goods (or, in some instances, dissimilar goods) for which the mark is registered. The relevant legislation is the Trade Marks Act 1994.
9. Copyright is the right to stop copying and distribution of a work. Examples of items which are potential copyright works are books, plays, music, paintings, films, sound recordings and broadcasts. The threshold requirement for originality, however, is set very low. Even lists of TV programmes or ingredients may be protected.
10. To qualify for protection, the work must be original (meaning 'not copied'), be recorded in a permanent form, and the author must be a 'qualifying person'. Copyright protection does not depend on registration but arises automatically once the work is created.

11. Copyright protection is generally granted for the life of the author plus 70 years. The copyright owner has a number of rights, for instance those concerning reproduction of the work; issuing copies of the work; performing the work in public; communicating the work to the public (whether by broadcast or the internet) or adapting the work. Note that independent creation is always a defence to copyright infringement. The relevant legislation is the Copyright, Designs and Patents Act 1988 (CDPA 1988).

## 1.4 European Influences on Intellectual Property

### 1.4.1 Patents

1. The European Patent Convention (EPC) of 1973 provides for a system made up of a single patent application and search. This does not result in a single patent – instead, the applicant is given a bundle of national patents.
2. In 1975 there was an attempt to create a single Community Patent (under the Community Patent Convention (CPC)), but this failed as the Convention did not enter into force.

### 1.4.2 Trade marks

European Community influence has occurred at two main levels. Firstly, a Community Trade Mark exists at Community level. Secondly, national trade mark law has been harmonised.

### 1.4.3 Copyright

1. Copyright law has been affected by Community law in a number of ways, but there has not been complete harmonisation of the entire subject area.
2. Rental and lending rights, databases, satellite broadcasts, and computer software have all been the subject of Directives.

The Information Society Directive deals with technological protection mechanisms. These Directives have been implemented into national law.

## 1.5 International Influences on Intellectual Property

1. Two international organisations have had a large impact on intellectual property – WIPO and TRIPS.
2. The start of the World Intellectual Propety Organization (WIPO) may be found in the Paris and Berne Conventions. The Paris Convention for the Protection of Intellectual Property 1883 covered trade marks, inventions and industrial designs, while the Berne Convention for the Protection of Literary and Artistic Works covered literary, artistic and musical works. Reciprocity is a central part of these agreements, whereby nationals of a Member State are to be treated in other Member States as if they were in their own.
3. WIPO was established as a UN agency in 1974 and now administers the above treaties among others. WIPO provides a forum in which members may debate issues and form future agreements.
4. 1996 saw an agreement between WIPO and the WTO for co-operation over Trade Related Aspects of Intellectual Property Rights (TRIPS). It was a result of long Uruguay Round discussions between 1988 and 1994.
5. The main provisions of TRIPS were that:
   - Copyright terms must extend to 50 years after the death of the author.
   - Copyright must be granted automatically and not based upon formality.
   - Computer programs must be regarded as 'literary works'.
   - National exceptions to copyright (such as 'fair use' in the United States) must be tightly constrained.

- Patents should be granted in all 'fields of technology', although some exceptions for certain public interests were allowed.
- In each state, intellectual property laws may not offer any benefits to local citizens which are not available to citizens of other TRIPs signatories by the principles of national treatment.

## 1.6 The Recent Reforms suggested by the UK Gowers Review

1. In December 2006, the Gowers Review suggested that a number of reforms could be made to intellectual property law. The main suggestions were as follows:
   (a) Patent law:
   - clarification of the research exemption in s60(5) Patents Act 1977;
   - support for the Community Patent;
   - a pilot scheme for cooperative examination of patent applications.

   (b) Trade marks:
   - a fast track system for trade marks for small businesses.

   (c) Copyright law:
   - private copying should be permitted;
   - there should be an exception for creative, transformative or derivative works (specifically in the Information Society Directive);
   - a defence of parody or pastiche should exist;
   - a provision for orphan works (works whose authors are untraceable).

# CHAPTER 2

# APPLYING FOR PATENTS AND EXCLUDED SUBJECT MATTER

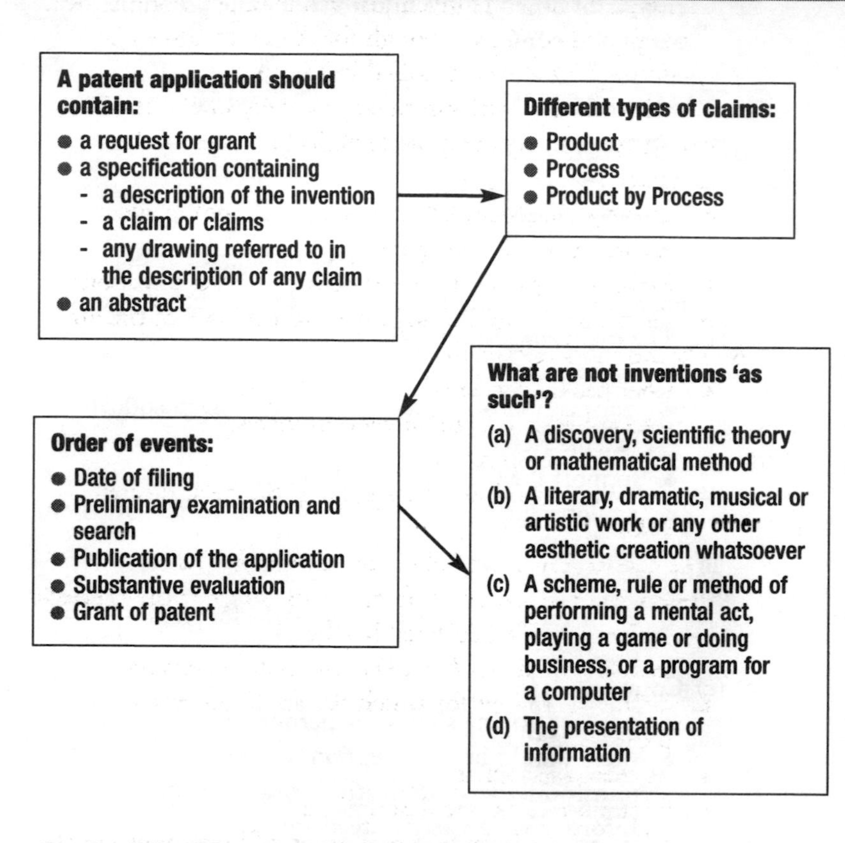

A patent application should contain:
a request for grant
a specification containing
- a description of the invention
- a claim or claims
- any drawing referred to in the description of any claim
an abstract
Different types of claims:
Product
Process
Product by Process
Order of events:
Date of filing
Preliminary examination and search
Publication of the application
Substantive evaluation
Grant of patent
What are not inventions 'as such'?
(a) A discovery, scientific theory or mathematical method
(b) A literary, dramatic, musical or artistic work or any other aesthetic creation whatsoever
(c) A scheme, rule or method of performing a mental act, playing a game or doing business, or a program for a computer
(d) The presentation of information


## 2.1 THE CONTENTS OF A PATENT APPLICATION

1. S14(2) Patents Act 1977:
   'Every application for a patent shall contain:
   (a) a request for the grant of a patent,

(b) a specification containing a description of the invention, a claim or claims, and any drawing referred to in the description of any claim, and

(c) an abstract.'

**2.** S14(3) Patents Act 1977 states that the specification:

'… shall disclose the invention in a manner which is clear enough and complete enough for the invention to be performed by a person skilled in the art.'

**3.** The abstract is a brief summary, normally of about 150 words, concerning the more technical features of the invention:

- used by the Patent Offices as a search tool in their examination of other patent applications;
- alerts third parties to the existence of an application;
- the abstract does not form part of the state of the art.

**4.** The description explains:

- what has been created;
- the problems that the invention solves;
- why it is important;
- how the invention differs to what has been created before.

The description essentially is there to enable us to understand the claims. In fact, it must support the claims, otherwise it may be declared invalid.

**5.** Under s14(5) Patents Act 1977, the claim needs to:

- define the matter for which the applicant seeks protection;
- be clear and concise;
- be supported by the description;
- relate to one invention or a group of inventions which are so linked as to form a single inventive concept.

There can be one main claim followed by subsidiary claims. Note narrower claims are not dependent on the wider claims. Amendment of the claims is possible. However, it is relatively limited because it can only be used to narrow the scope of claims (which you might do to avoid infringement).

## 2.2 DIFFERENT TYPES OF CLAIMS

### 2.2.1 Product claims

1. The first type recognised under UK law. It provides protection over physical entities such as products, apparatuses, devices and substances.
2. Product claims confer protection over all uses of that product, no matter how the product was derived.

### 2.2.2 Process claims

1. These protect activities or actions (such as methods, processes, or uses).
2. Sometimes a product per se claim isn't possible, so this is another route

### 2.2.3 Product by process claims

1. A hybrid. For example, X made by process Y.
2. Not the same as a process claim, for a patentee can define the monopoly claimed so as to disclaim products made by a particular process or only disclaim products which do not have the features of products made by a particular process. **Note** the EPO Technical Board of Appeal, which states it does not support product by process claims. It is only acceptable as a manner of claiming structurally indefinable product claims or where a product cannot be defined by its features. However, the UK Court of Appeal has said there are no such limits under the Patents Act 1977 or EPC (e.g. *Kirin Amgen*).

### 2.2.4 The drawings

1. Along with the description, these may be used to interpret the claims. The Patent Office provides very clear rules as to how to provide the drawings.

## 2.3 Applying for a Patent – Procedure for Application

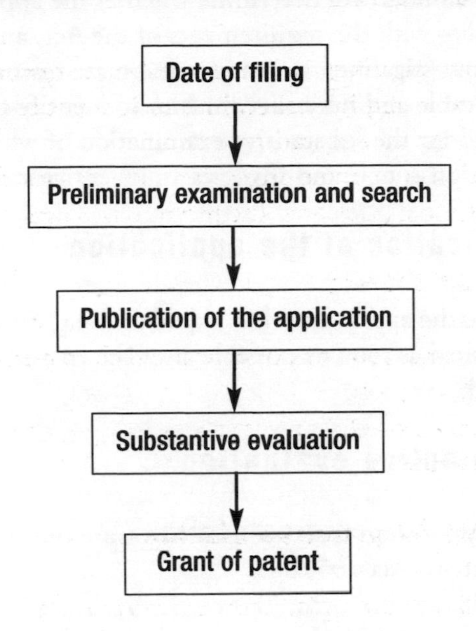


### 2.3.1 Date of filing

1. The date of filing for a patent will be the date on which certain (minimum) formalities are satisfied, the rest being supplied later. The filing date is treated as the priority date, unless the application is based on an earlier Convention application, in which case this will be the priority date.
2. Note that in regard to restrictions on filing abroad by UK residents, permits to first-file abroad will need only be sought for applications relating to military technology or those prejudicial to national security or public safety.

### 2.3.2 Preliminary examination and search

1. The examiner will determine whether the application complies with the requirements of the Act, and then make such investigations as in his opinion are reasonably practicable and necessary for him to identify the documents needed for the substantive examination of whether the invention is new and involves an inventive step.

### 2.3.3 Publication of the application

1. Where the application has a date of filing it shall be published as soon as possible after the end of the prescribed period.

### 2.3.4 Substantive evaluation

1. The application is scrutinised to ensure that it complies with the Patents Act 1977.

### 2.3.5 Grant of patent

1. Where the application succeeds and the correct fee has been paid, then the Comptroller will grant the applicant a patent. The duration is for 20 years from the filing date, and continuation of the grant is subject to renewal fees.
2. The comptroller or Courts may now exercise their discretion in allowing an amendment after grant. A new section in the Patents Act 2004 (s2) requires the Comptroller and Courts to have regard to any relevant principles under the European Patent Convention.

## 2.4 THE STEPS THAT MUST BE GONE THROUGH TO GET A PATENT IN TERMS OF VALIDITY

**1.** The following questions should be asked, namely:

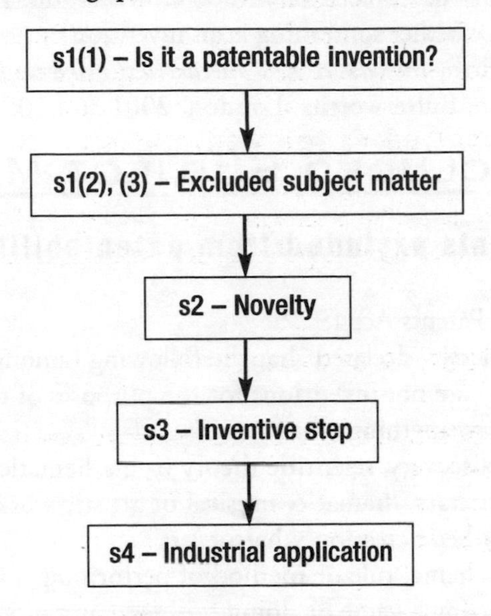


**2.** Sections 2 to 4 will be dealt with in the next two chapters.

## 2.5 IS SOMETHING AN INVENTION?

**1.** S1(1) Patents Act 1977 – A patent may be granted only for an invention in respect of which the following conditions are satisfied:

(a) the invention is new;
(b) it involves an inventive step;
(c) it is capable of industrial application;
(d) the grant of a patent for it is not excluded under sections (2) and (3) below.

2. Nonetheless, an invention is defined later on in the Patents Act, namely s2, s3 and s4. The definition within s1(1) is nebulous:
   '... the failure to define "invention" is, probably, not merely excusable but even justifiable ... Second, it is hard to conceive of a precise definition ... Third, one rarely needs to know whether something is an invention or not.' (Philips and Firth, *Introduction to Intellectual Property Law,* 4th edition, Butterworths, London, 2001 at 4.10.)

## 2.6 Excluded Subject Matter

### 2.6.1 Patents excluded from patentability

1. S1(2) Patents Act 1977:
   'It is hereby declared that the following (among other things) are not inventions for the purposes of this Act, that is to say, anything which consists of:
   (a) a discovery, scientific theory or mathematical method;
   (b) a literary, dramatic, musical or artistic work or any other aesthetic creation whatsoever;
   (c) a scheme, rule or method of performing a mental act, playing a game or doing business, or a program for a computer;
   (d) the presentation of information.'
2. This has a proviso:
   '... the foregoing provision shall prevent anything from being treated as an invention for the purposes of this Act only to the extent that a patent or application for a patent relates to that thing as such.'
3. This section is based on Article 52(2) of the EPC:
   'The following in particular shall not be regarded as inventions within the meaning of paragraph 1:
   (a) discoveries, scientific theories and mathematical methods;
   (b) aesthetic creations;

(c) schemes, rules and methods of performing mental acts, playing games or doing business, and programs for computers;
(d) presentation of information.'

4. This similarly has a proviso in Article 52(3):
'The provisions of paragraph 2 shall exclude patentability of the subject matter or activities referred to in that provision only to the extent to which a European patent relates to such subject matter or activities as such.'

### 2.6.2 How should the term 'as such' be defined?

1. There are three potential approaches:
   (a) take an overall analysis;
   (b) focus on the character of the invention and ask whether that is technical;
   (c) if the claim contains excluded matter then an overall analysis of the invention's contribution to the art and whether this has 'technical character'.
2. The whole contents approach was used by the Court of Appeal in *Merrill Lynch* (1989), following the EPO case of *VICOM* (1987).
3. This decision expressly rejected the approach in *Wards Application* (1912) where if novelty lay in an element not within the exclusions, then the device could be patentable.
4. The approach in *Merrill Lynch* (1989) meant that matter excluded by s1(2) could contribute the inventive step required to make an invention patentable. There should be a new technical result, the result itself not being excluded by s1(2).
   - For instance, in *Re Wang Laboratories Inc's Application* (1991) a computer-related invention was excluded from patentability.
   - In *Fujitsu Ltd's Application* (1977) there was a computer programmed to model synthetic crystal structure and the issue was whether there was any technical contribution.

- *R v Hutchins Application* (2002) relates to claims to a computer program. The examiner advised that the invention was unpatentable because it related only to a program.

5. Also note *Pension Benefits Systems* (2002). 'Apparatus' claims to software operating a pension scheme by calculating amounts due on standard factors were not disallowed on the basis of the exclusion, although claims to the methods of making the calculations were rejected as computer programs as such. In the apparatus claims the mere presence of a computer served to provide a technical element, although the computer did not contribute to the system and merely implemented it. However, no inventive step could be shown. Rather than looking at the contribution made by the invention and determining whether this was technical, the Board focused on the character of the invention.

## 2.7 THE SPECIFIC EXCLUSIONS

### 2.7.1 Discoveries, scientific theories and mathematical methods as such

1. A discovery must be distinguished from an invention: 'Discovery adds to the amount of human knowledge, but it does so only by lifting a veil and disclosing something which before had been unseen or dully seen … Invention … must be an act which results in a new product, or a new result, or a new process, or a new combination for producing an old product or an old result.' (Buckley J in *Reynolds v Herbert Smith* (1913).)

### 2.7.2 Scientific theory and mathematical methods

1. Scientific theory:
'A scientific theory – this means that Einstein's theory of relativity and the various accounts of black holes in space cannot be inventions. This exclusion is eminently sensible

since, being no more than hypothesis or explanations as to how physical events occur, theories cannot as such be realistically exploited industrially. On the other hand, a device which operates through the practical application of a scientific theory will be regarded an invention.' (Philips and Firth, *Introduction to Intellectual Property Law*, 4th edition, Butterworths, London, 2001 at 4.11.)

2. Mathematical methods are to be treated in the same way as discoveries. A device for mathematical methods which performs those methods will be patentable *(Re Gale* (1991)).

### 2.7.3 Literary, dramatic, musical or artistic works as such

1. These things are primarily best left within the scope of copyright, see Part 1 CDPA 1988.
2. However, this does not mean that the other aspects of an invention may not be patentable (*Re ESP's Application* (1945)).

### 2.7.4 The presentation of information as such

1. *Pitman's Application* (1969) – a claim was made to a layout of words on a printed page, which conveyed visually to the reader the correct way of pronouncing the words. This achieved a patent because the printed sheets were designed to be used in a reading machine (a technical device) and had a mechanical purpose.

### 2.7.5 Schemes, rules and methods of performing mental acts, playing games or doing business, and programs for computers as such

1. EPO guidelines point to:
   - schemes for learning a language;
   - solving a crossword;
   - rules for a card game; or

- a scheme of office management,

unless they also involve a novel apparatus.

### 2.7.6 Schemes, rules and methods

1. Schemes for performance of a mental act – *W's Application* (1914) – an arrangement for navigation buoys – merely a system for arranging known objects.
2. *Hiller's Application* (1969) – a plan for arranging underground utility cables.

### 2.7.7 Methods of doing business

1. *Merrill Lynch* (1989) – Court of Appeal held a share trading system operated by a computer unpatentable.
2. *Patterson/Queuing System* (1995) – system for handling customer queuing.
3. *Pension Benefits Systems* (2002) – a business method invention is only patentable if it can be shown that it has technical character.

### 2.7.8 Programs for computers

1. *VICOM* (1987) – An application where the subject matter of the invention is the technical effect produced by the operation of a computer program. The patent is granted in relation to the technical effect and not the computer program as such, and it makes no difference whether or not the inventive step resides in the computer program itself.
2. It also confirms that there should be no distinction between modes of storage.
3. There has to be some technical effect that is novel and non-obvious. If the only purpose of the program is to run on a computer than it cannot be patented. This was followed by the EPO in *IBM Document Abstracting* (1990). This made a general distinction: whether the computer program creates a technical *industrial* effect, or merely an *intellectual* effect.

4. In *IBM Computer Programs* (1990), the above approach was followed. However, the EPO Technical Board of Appeal also held that a computer program that has the ability to cause a predetermined technical effect was not excluded from patentability under the EPC.
5. Note that the proposed Directive concerning the patentability of software was defeated in the European Parliament during July 2005 (by 648 votes to 14). It will not be re-introduced.

### 2.7.9 Mental acts

1. These are excluded under s1(2)(c) Patents Act 1977.
   - Text editing – if an application uses the same steps as a mental process it will not be patentable – (Case T-38/86) *IBM Text Clarity Processing* (1990).
   - If, on the other hand, it involves a technical step, it is *prima facie* patentable – *IBM Editable Document Form* (1995).
   - Expert Systems – the UK has consistently held that an operation that could be carried out by humans is not patentable – *Wang Laboratories Application* (1991) (even if the act is much faster than can be carried out unaided by humans).

## 2.8 General Exceptions to Patentability

### 2.8.1 Key legislation to consider

1. EPC Art 53(a):
   'Inventions the publication or exploitation of which would be contrary to "*ordre public*" or morality, provided that the exploitation shall not be deemed to be so contrary merely because it is prohibited by law or regulation in some or all of the Contracting States.'

2. S1(3) Patents Act 1977:
   'A patent shall not be granted for an invention the commercial exploitation of which would be contrary to public policy or morality.'
   (Since changed, the old s1(3)(a) mentioned offensive, immoral or anti-social behaviour.)
3. Directive 98/44/EC – The Biotechnology Directive:
   Article 6 – rules out patents whose commercial exploitation would be contrary to:
   '*ordre public* or morality; however, exploitation shall not be deemed to be so contrary merely because it is prohibited by law or regulation.'
   Article 6(2) provides a non exclusive list of things not patentable:
   - processes for cloning human beings;
   - processes for modifying the germ line genetic identity of human beings;
   - uses of human embryos for industrial or commercial purposes;
   - processes for modifying the genetic identity of animals which are likely to cause them suffering without any substantial medical benefit to man or animal, and also animals resulting from such processes.

### 2.8.2 Key cases to consider

1. There are some key cases to consider in this area.
2. *Harvard (Onco Mouse)* (2003) (Technical Board of Appeal of the EPO):
   - Article 53(a) will only apply in exceptional circumstances.
   - When it is applied, 'extreme positions', e.g. possible abuses of the invention, would not be taken into account.
   - *Ordre public* and morality should be assessed primarily by looking at laws/regulations common to most European countries.

3. A similar approach was followed in *Plant Genetic Systems* (1995), again by the Technical Board of Appeal – although it may be difficult, Art 53(a) may not be disregarded by the EPO when assessing patentability.
4. That approach should be contrasted with that of the EPO Opposition Division (lower in the hierarchy than the Technical Board of Appeal).
5. In *Howard Florey* (1995), it was said that the EPO was not the right institution to decide on fundamental ethical questions: that there are plenty of other fields that could also be objectionable to parts of the public.
6. *Plant Genetic Systems* (1995) also decided that opinion polls should not be decisive, which has been described as splitting up empirical evidence from the use of Art 53(a).

### 2.8.3 Biological subject matter

1. The key element here is the difference between something found in nature and a process for reproducing that substance in the laboratory. In *Onco-Mouse* (2003) the Opposition Division said:
   - no doubt that living matter and in particular plants and animals could be patented;
   - the exclusion was limited to varieties only, and that it could not be extended to animals in general.
2. Note the Patents Act 1977, Schedule A2(3)(f): 'any variety of animal or plant or an essentially biological process for the production of animals or plants, not being a micro-biological or other technical process or the product of such a process.'
3. *Onco-Mouse* (1990) held that a genetically engineered mouse is not an animal variety. In regard to plant varieties, note the International Convention for the Protection of New Varieties of Plants (UPOV). The original 1961 regime granted protection in plant varieties. It was decided that the EPC should be mutually exclusive with UPOV, hence the

exclusion, but the necessity was removed by the 1991 UPOV revisions.

4. In *Plant Genetic Systems* (1995), the Board of Appeal said that 'the concept of plant variety under Article 53(b) refers to any plant grouping within a single botanical taxon [or classification] of the lowest known rank'. Thus plant cells as such, 'cannot be considered to fall under the definition of plant or plant variety'. A plant variety 'is characterised by at least one single transmissible characteristic distinguishing it from other plant groupings and which is sufficiently homogeneous and stable in its relevant characteristics.'
5. *Novartis* (2000) follows Art 4(2) of the Biotechnology Directive:
   '... [I]nventions which concern plants ... shall be patentable if the technical feasibility of the invention is not confined to a particular plant ... variety'.
6. In *Novartis*, the enlarged board of appeal said:
   - 'a claim wherein specific plant varieties are not individually claimed is not excluded from patentability under Art 53(b), even though it embraces plant varieties.'
   - The extent of the exclusion for patents is the obverse of the availability of plant variety rights, and that plant varieties are only granted for specific plant varieties (and not for technical teachings).
7. Note that 'Essentially Biological Processes' concern only the production of animals or plants, and not death or destruction of them.
8. It only applies if a process is 'essentially biological', which, in the words of the Biotechnology Directive, is if it 'consists entirely of natural phenomena such as crossing or selection' (Art 2(2)). A degree of intervention is needed. In *Lubrizol* (1990) there were the steps of:
   (i) selecting parent plants and crossing;
   (ii) resulting hybrids being selected;
   (iii) the parent plants then being cloned.

9. The Board of Appeal decided this was *not* an 'essentially biological process'.
10. Following *Novartis* (2000), although the case is not clear as to how to interpret the phrase, we do now know that purely biological processes are essentially biological.
11. In relation to micro-biological processes, we can turn to *Plant Genetic Systems* (1995). This confirmed that a microbiological process is immune from being 'essentially biological' simply because a microbiological step is involved.
12. Note however, on the facts of the case, the introductory step of transforming plant cells or tissues with recombinant DNA *was* microbiological. However, Art 53(b) has been qualified by Art 6(1)(f) of the Biotechnology Directive so that if an invention is microbiological *or technical* then it will not be caught by the exclusion.

# CHAPTER 3
# NOVELTY

The order of assessing patentability:

- s1(1) – is it a patentable invention?
- s1(2), (3) – excluded subject matter
- s2 – novelty
- s3 – inventive step
- s4 – industrial application

A patented invention should not be part of the prior art. Examples of the Prior Art are:

- books
- oral communication
- prior use

Where there is an enabling disclosure it is assessed from the eyes of:

(i) a person skilled in the art
(ii) who has common general knowledge
(iii) which he or she may use to get the invention to work and
(iv) recognise and rectify errors in the description of the invention.

## 3.1 THE STEPS TO OBTAIN A PATENT

### 3.1.1 The steps that must be gone through to get a patent in terms of validity

1. In the last chapter, we mentioned which steps are required to obtain a patent. These were:

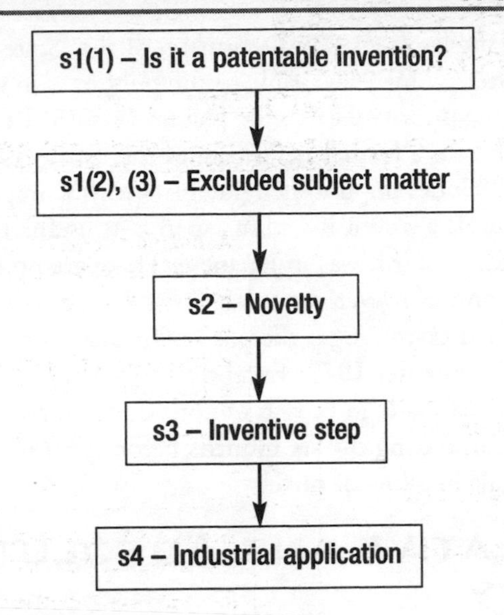


2. This chapter will consider 'novelty' in s2.

### 3.1.2 The purpose of 'novelty'

1. The purpose of novelty means that the conferral of a monopoly will do two main things:
   (i) create an incentive;
   (ii) in exchange for requiring the patentee to divulge new (novel) details of the invention.

## 3.2 LEGISLATIVE PROVISIONS

### 3.2.1 Definitions

1. In order to consider the nature of novelty, it is necessary to consider the statutory definition:
   'S2(1) Patents Act 1977: An invention [is] … new if it does not form part of the state of the art'. In other words, to be novel it must not be part of the 'state of the art'.

2. S2(2) Patents Act 1977: Definition of the 'State of the Art'. 'all matter ... made available to the public ... in any way' before the priority date of the patent. In s2(3) Patents Act 1977 there is a further definition of the 'State of the Art' which includes unpublished patents which is important, for example a patent issued in Japan is as useful as a patent in England, even if it was in Japanese! There are no geographical restrictions. However, note that unpublished patents are not used when examining if there is an inventive step.
3. S2(4) Patents Act 1977: Exception to loss of novelty: Disclosures made in breach of confidence/international exhibition during the six months before priority date will not result in a loss of novelty.

## 3.3 Relative and Absolute Novelty

1. Note that in the UK there is absolute and not relative novelty. Relative novelty existed under the 1949 Act. Also under the 1949 Act, anticipation through use did not need an enabling disclosure, but anticipation through publication did.

## 3.4 Identification of the Prior Art

1. Prior art may take any form, provided it is before the priority date of the application. Note that in the UK there is no 'grace period'. This is a period during which prior to filing they may be able to practice their inventions (this would in practice increase patent term). This does, however, exist in the US where it is of six months' duration. Note also that the key question is whether information *could* be accessed, not whether it *has actually* been accessed.

### 3.4.1 Examples of the prior art

1. What examples are there of the prior art?
   - **Oral communications** – *Visx Inc v Nidek Co Ltd* (1999) – the burden of proof lies with the person alleging prior disclosure.
   - **Books** – *Lang v Gisbourne* (1862) – question is whether, and what, information was available – not whether the book was sold.
   - **Prior use** – *Pall Corporation v Commercial Hydraulics (Bedford) Ltd* (1989) held that delivering samples in confidence to persons who knew that they were experimental did not make the invention available to the public for the purposes of s2(1) and did not, therefore, prejudice the novelty of the invention. See also *Quantel v Spaceward* (1990), which held that use during PC video card demonstrations did not anticipate use, because in that case the use did not show how the product worked.

### 3.4.2 Public use

1. What does 'public' use have to be?
   - *Windsurfer International v Tabur Marine* (1985) – the Court of Appeal held that a 12-year-old boy, who built a sailboard and used it in public for a few weekends at a caravan site at Hayling Island in Hampshire, had effectively anticipated a later patent for a sailboard.
   - *Lux v Pike* (1993) – Testing of traffic light control system in public. Field trials of a traffic light control system were carried out before the relevant filing. Defendant argued that the invention had been made available to the public because a prototype had been used and it did not matter if the feature claimed by the patentee had been seen. Aldous J stated 'it is settled law that there is no need to prove that anybody actually saw the disclosure provided the relevant disclosure was in public'.

2. In *Availability to the Public* (1993), it was questioned whether a person skilled in the art might need to be 'pushed' into a particular direction. The case suggests that everything is public provided it is 'without undue burden'.
3. In *Milliken Denmark AS v Walk Off Mats* (1996), Jacob J outlined that although the rule may seem harsh, it provides a bright line test. Anticipation would seemingly occur even if the earlier skilled person would not appreciate the benefit of the invention.
4. *Union Carbide* (1991) – once the information has been identified, the essential question is what this teaches the skilled addressee.

## 3.5 Enabling Disclosure

1. This should be assessed from the perspective of the ordinary skilled person, *not* someone of exceptional skill and knowledge, or, in the words of Jacob J, 'a world champion' (*Synthonb BV v Smithkline Beecham PLC* (2002)). Once subject matter is disclosed, the key issue is whether the person skilled in the art is prepared to carry out trial and error experiments to get the invention to work.
2. It is usual to read the specification from the perspective of the addressee:

**(i) A person skilled in the art;**
**(ii) who has common general knowledge;**
**(iii) which he or she may use to get the invention to work;**
**(iv) and even to recognise and rectify errors in the description of the invention.**

3. One of the main cases in this field is *General Tire & Rubber Co v Firestone Tyre and Rubber Co Ltd* (1972). This concerned the validity of Firestone's patent for making oil-extended rubber for tyres, which had been challenged by General Tire. It was held that to anticipate the claim, the prior publication must contain a clear and unmistakable

direction to do what the patentee claimed to have invented. 'A signpost, however clear, upon the road to the patentee's invention will not suffice. The prior inventor must be clearly shown to have planted his flag at the precise destination before the patentee …'

4. The approach in *General Tire* may be summarised as follows:

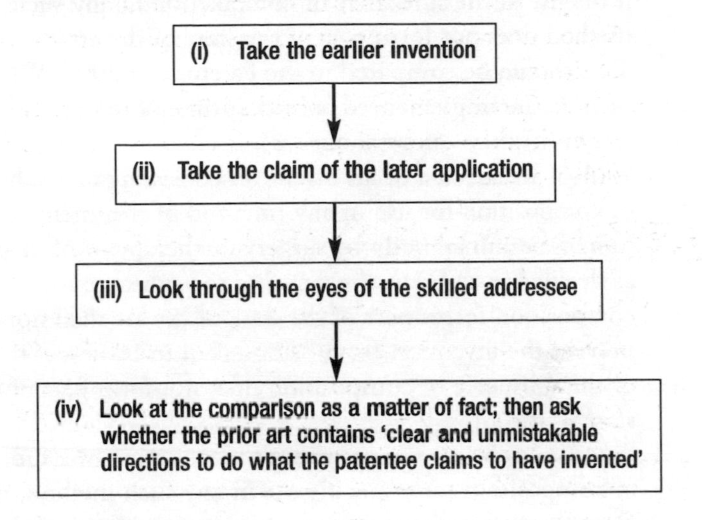
(i) Take the earlier invention
(ii) Take the claim of the later application
(iii) Look through the eyes of the skilled addressee
(iv) Look at the comparison as a matter of fact; then ask whether the prior art contains 'clear and unmistakable directions to do what the patentee claims to have invented'

5. In *Union Carbide Corp v BP Chemicals Ltd* (1998) Jacobs J in the Patent Court said that a direction in a prior publication not to do something was not the same thing as being told to do something. In *Hoechst Celanese v BP Chemicals* (1998) it was said that '… if [the skilled man] would find a teaching implicit, it is indeed taught'. Finally, in *Asahi Kasei Kogyo's Application* (1991), it was outlined that the disclosure must enable the skilled person to work the invention.

## 3.6 NEW USES OF OLD THINGS

1. Old inventions may be patentable if the claims are directed to a new use. The key section is s2(6) Patents Act 1977:

'S2(6) In the case of an invention consisting of a substance or composition for use in a method of treatment of the human or animal body by surgery or therapy or of diagnosis practised on the human or animal body, the fact that the substance or composition forms part of the state of the art shall not prevent the invention from being taken to be new if the use of the substance or composition in any such method does not form part of the state of the art.'

This should be compared to the Patents Act 2004. When the sections are implemented (which at time of writing they have not been) they will replace s2(6).

'S4A(3) In the case of an invention consisting of a substance or composition for use in any [method of treatment of the human or animal body by surgery or therapy or of diagnosis as detailed in s4A(1)], the fact that the substance or composition forms part of the state of the art shall not prevent the invention from being taken to be new if the use of the substance or composition does not form part of the state of the art.'

'S4A(4) In the case of an invention consisting of a substance or composition for a specific use in any such method, the fact that the substance or composition forms part of the state of the art shall not prevent the invention from being taken to be new if that specific use does not form part of the state of the art.'

2. Note that the revised law permits the patenting of new uses of known chemical substances when used in a medical context, novelty arising via the new *purpose* even though the purpose itself (medical treatment) is regarded as being excluded (on policy grounds) from being patentable.
3. On face value, the old law only applied to first use, but the EPO extended it to cover second and subsequent uses (see below). The literal approach found some support in the UK case of *John Wyeth & Bros Ltd's Application: Schering AG'S Application* (1985).

However, in the end the court followed the enlarged board of appeal EPO in *Eisai* (1979-85).

- Claims directed to the use of a product for the treatment of an illness were equivalent to a method for treatment and therefore excluded.
- Claims for the use of a product for the manufacture of a medicament for a new therapeutic use were not lacking in novelty.

**4.** In *Pffizer Ltd's Patent* (2001) it was held that the method must be effective to achieve the new treatment and not simply be a placebo effect. Laddie J also accepted that if a combination of compounds is used to treat a disease, then each is used for the treatment of the disease. Thus, second uses could be patentable.

**5.** *Mobil Oil* (1996) concerned a claim based on the discovery that an existing compound used for preventing rust was also effective as a lubricant, the example of a compound that had been previously known and used as a plant growth regulator was discussed. This suggested that the new use of a known compound may reflect a newly discovered technical effect which could be considered as a functional feature of the relevant claim. If that technical feature had not previously been made available to the public the claim would be novel (even though it had already inherently taken place).

**6.** *Mobil Oil* was followed by *Bristol-Myers Squibb v Norton* (2001). This concerned a patent for making a medication for treating cancer by administering the drug over a period of three hours, thereby reducing neutropenia. It was already known that administering it over three hours was as good as administering it over 24 hours, but it was not known that neutropenia was less under the three hour regime. The Court of Appeal accepted the correctness of *Eisai*, and confirmed the Swiss type claim was possible. However, here the quicker time was in fact a discovery and the Court of Appeal said it must be a new therapeutic use or purpose. As regards *Mobil Oil*, Aldous LJ said it differed from *Eisai*. *Eisai* concerned the link between EPC Arts 52(4) and 54(5), whereas *Mobil Oil* was trying to deal with Art 69 and a construction of claims.

CHAPTER 4

# INVENTIVE STEP AND INDUSTRIAL APPLICATION

**There are different approaches to assessing inventive step:**
- **The EPO use the 'problem and solution' approach**
- **The UK uses the approach of 'windsurfing'**

**Industrial application has a few areas of concern:**
- **surgery and therapy**
- **cosmetic treatment**
- **treatment for infestations**

## 4.1 LEGISLATIVE PROVISIONS

1. S3 Patents Act 1977:
   'An invention shall be taken to involve an inventive step if it is not obvious to a person skilled in the art, having regard to any matter which forms part of the state of the art by virtue only of s2(2) above (and disregarding s2(3) above).'
   This corresponds to Art 56 EPC.
2. An 'Inventive Step' is something that is not obvious to the person skilled in the art. It exists to prevent every single improvement being patentable – which could impede legitimate work. In contrast to novelty, this test is qualitative, because it involves assessing the merit of the claims.

## 4.2 ATTEMPTS AT DEFINITION

1. Note the various attempts at defining what this means:
   - *General Tire v Firestone* (1972) – 'very plain'; and
   - *Vickers v Siddell* (1890) – 'so obvious that it would at once occur to anyone acquainted with the subject and desirous of accomplishing the end'.

## 4.3 DIFFERENT APPROACHES

1. The EPO and UK use different approaches:

- **The EPO uses the 'problem and solution' approach.**

- **The UK uses the approach of 'Windsurfing'.**

### 4.3.1 The EPO approach

1. The problem and solution approach asks whether the solution to the problem was obvious to the person skilled in the art. The EPO settled for it after a need for what it called an 'objective, economical, and transparent approach'.
2. In *ICI* [1979-85] the proposition was put forward that the approach was mandatory. Note, however, the technical board of appeal later suggested that there was no legal basis for this – *Alcan (Aluminium Alloys)*.

**3.** A general breakdown of the approach:
In the *'Szabo Maxims'* case (1995):

**(i) A single starting point in the prior art should be selected for examination of the inventive step.**

↓

**(ii) Any source may be used as the starting point (of the prior art).**

↓

**(iii) Problem must be defined without knowledge of the invention, and the solution is to be identified in terms of the effects achieved.**

↓

**(iv) Skilled person assumed to search for secondary sources ONLY after the specific problem or problems have been recognised.**

↓

**(v) He must find the modifying features in a single secondary source.**

↓

**(vi) This combination must been done per favourable/discouraging circumstances (and a long list of other relevant criteria – including things like: commercial success; overcoming difficulties; satisfaction of long need; failure and unsuccessful attempts of others; increased performance; cheaper or more economic production; etc.).**

## 4.3.2 The approach of the UK

**1.** The key case for the UK approach is *Windsurfing International v Tabur Marine* [1985].

**2.** The '*Windsurfer*' approach comprises of four stages, in which the court should:

**(i) identify the inventive concept embodied in the patent in suit;**

↓

**(ii) assume the mantle of the skilled but unimaginative addressee;**

↓

**(iii) identify the differences between the generally known matter and the subject matter of the patent;**

↓

**(iv) ask if those differences constitute steps which would have been obvious to the skilled man.**

3. The approach has been reaffirmed by the Court of Appeal in *Molnlycke AB v Procter & Gamble Ltd (No. 5)* [1994].
4. It is possible to create a mosaic of information for the addressee, unlike novelty. It is fitting to the nature of the inquiry. Note that if an invention combines two documents from *neighbouring* fields it may be obvious. Unlike novelty, furthermore, obviousness ignores patent applications which have already been filed but are yet to be published.

## 4.4 The Skilled Addressee

### 4.4.1 Some examples of addressees

1. In *Dyson v Hoover* (2002) it was said, due to the facts of the case, that the 'notional addressee is to be regarded as a graduate or HND engineer in either mechanical or electrical engineering (probably a team of both) with a few years practical experience'.
2. In *General Tire & Rubber Co v Firestone Tyre and Rubber Co Ltd* (1972), 'it is common ground that the skilled addressee is in effect a composite entity – a typical chief compounder and a typical scientific adviser as found in the organisation of any company manufacturing tyres on a large scale'.

3. Note that in *Rockwater v Technip* (2004), it was said that 'it is settled that this man, if real, would be very boring – a *nerd*'.
4. The common characteristic of the addressee is that they be unimaginative and uninventive. However, note the following points:
   - In *Re Genentech's Patent* (1989) Puchas LJ recognised that the 'person skilled in the art' must have inventive capacity (but note the Court of Appeal decided that the traditional model was unworkable in the exceptional circumstances in question).
   - The case concerned the question of whether the production of an activator for blood clotting was a breakthrough or simply a development of previous recombinant DNA technology.
   - The facts of the case are important.
5. As noted in *Dyson v Hoover* (2002) a skilled addressee may be imbued with certain prejudices. There may be evidence of this in the trade or product development in general. If a certain avenue of thought has never been persued (because it is thought of as not worthy), then it would be reasonable to expect the addressee to think the same.
6. The addressee knows what is called 'the common general knowledge'. In *General Tire & Rubber Co v Firestone Tyre and Rubber Co Ltd* (1972) it is a 'commonsense approach to the practical question of what would in fact be known to an appropriately skilled addressee – the sort of man, good at his job, that could be found in real life'. It may include the knowledge of his area and may also include that which can be found in encyclopaedias and standard dictionaries (although this does not mean that everything contained within will necessarily be within the common general knowledge).
7. Whether there is an inventive step or not is decided without hindsight – *Haberman v Jackel* (1999). However, imbued prejudices held by a skilled addressee could blind the addressee in regard to a particular solution – *Dyson v Hoover* (2002).

**8.** It is important to consider the evidence of expert witnesses when determining whether a particular step is obvious, *but importantly,* note that the skilled addressee is not the same person – *Beloit Technologies v Valmet* (1997).

### 4.4.2 Claims

**1.** Points concerning the claims (regards interpretation):
- The claims are defined in light of the skilled addressee.
- In *Dyson v Hoover* (2002), it was said that the court 'construes objectively, but adopting the mantle of the notional addressee, in light of the common general knowledge'.
- The claim is initially *construed* by the court without regard to the cited prior art. This is *not* the same as claim interpretation which happens afterward. Initial construal is merely an initial reading.

## 4.5 The Prior Art

**1.** Note that the meaning of the prior art (in the context of inventive step) is largely the same as that discussed above for novelty, except for:
(i) Patent applications that have priority over the application in suit, but have not yet been published, are *not* included (*BASF/Metal Refining* (1979-85)).
(ii) It is possible to combine information together from different sources.

## 4.6 Capable of Industrial Application – Legislative Provisions

1. S4 Patents Act 1977:
   'An invention shall be taken to be capable of industrial application if it can be made or used in any kind of industry, including agriculture.'
   [This corresponds to Art 57 EPC.]
2. The phrase was new to the 1977 Patents Act: previously, the invention had to represent a new method of manufacture. The new approach is broader and more favourable to patentees than the equivalent in the 1949 Patents Act. The new requirement reflects the practical nature of patent law, which requires that the invention should be something which can be made industrially or relate to an industrial process.
3. The 'industrial application' step is rarely of issue, but has become an area of debate concerning methods of treatment.

## 4.7 Methods of Treatment to the Human or Animal Body

### 4.7.1 Industrial application

1. There is a limit to 'industrial application' in the Patents Act:
   'S4(2) An invention of a method of treatment of the human or animal body by surgery or therapy or of diagnosis practised on the human or animal body shall not be taken to be capable of industrial application.'
   'S4(3) 4(2) shall not prevent a product consisting of a substance or composition being treated as capable of industrial application merely because it is invented for any such use or method.'
   [The equivalent is Art 52(4) in the EPC.]

The exclusion does not extend to products consisting of substances or compositions used in any such methods (s4(3)).

2. The section ensures that GP's and vets are not inhibited by patents. It applies to methods: it does not affect surgical, therapeutic, or diagnostic substances and compositions (e.g. drugs, apparatuses or products).

### 4.7.2 Surgery and therapy

1. Both surgery and therapy have been broadly defined. Surgery includes non-invasive procedures (e.g. repositioning) and invasive procedures. Therapy may include prophylactic treatments.
2. Surgery has had a wide definition – in *Shell* (1999) it was held to be 'The branch of medicine concerned with the healing of disease, accidental injury, or bodily defects by operating on the living body'.
3. The method of treatment has similarly been given a wide interpretation by *Unilever (Davis' Application)* (1983).

### 4.7.3 Cosmetic treatment

1. Cosmetic treatment falls outside the exclusion (as it is not carried out for noble reasons) and so is patentable. See *Roussel-UCLAF* (1987).
2. This is also the case with pregnancy and conception. See *Schering AG's Application* (1971).

### 4.7.4 Treatment for infestations

1. If it can be shown that there is a treatment for, e.g., ridding a body of lice, then this may be patentable if it is accepted as a treatment towards ridding the body of human lice – *Stafford Miller's Application* (1984).

2. Note though the EPO in *Wellcome/Pigs I* (1998) – the Board of Appeal considered a method of treating mange in pigs by the application of a composition of pesticides to the surface of a pigs body to be a method of treating an animal body and excluded.
3. Note also *Stafford Miller* was decided under the 1949 Act.

CHAPTER 5

# INFRINGEMENT AND DEFENCES

**There is primary and secondary infringement**

**Different requirements exist to establish infringement for:**

- **product patents**
- **process patents**
- **product by process patents**

**The main test for assessing similarity of claims comes from *Improver v Remington* (1990):**

**(i) Would a person with practical knowledge and experience understand that strict compliance with a particular descriptive word or phrase appearing in a claim was intended by the patentee to be an essential requirement of the invention so that any variant would fall outside the monopoly claimed, even though it could have no material effect upon the way the invention worked. That question does not arise where the variant would in fact have a material effect upon the way the invention worked.**

**(ii) At the date of publication of the specification was it obvious to the informed reader that this was so?**

**(iii) Where it is not obvious, in the light of the then-existing knowledge, the reader is to assume that the patentee thought at the time of the specification that he had good reason for limiting his monopoly so strictly, unless it is clear otherwise it could have been intended by the patentee.**

**Defences for infringement include among others:**

- **bringing the validity of the original patent into question**
- **honest concurrent use**
- **private non-commerical use**
- **experimental purposes**

## 5.1 Infringement

1. Infringement and validity are actionable in the UK courts. This is different to Germany, where validity may only be heard by the Patent Office.
2. In the UK, it is common practice when infringement is alleged to counterclaim that the patent is invalid.
3. In the UK it is now possible to obtain a non-binding ruling. The opinions were introduced in s13 Patents Act 2004 and came into force on 1 October 2005. They are designed to provide a quick and cheap alternative to litigation in court.
4. Anyone can request an opinion directly from the Patent Office for £200. This includes the patentee himself. Other parties can file observations. A Patent Office examiner will consider all the points and observations raised in the request before issuing an opinion. The opinion is not legally binding and can be reviewed by the requester within three months of the opinion.

## 5.2 Types of Infringement

1. S60 Patents Act 1977 defines the main types of infringement. It is based on Art 25 CPC. Infringement is either:
   - primary; or
   - secondary.

### 5.2.1 Primary infringement

1. Within s60(1) there are three main types of infringement:
   (a) where the invention is a product, he makes, disposes of, offers to dispose of, uses or imports the product or keeps it whether for disposal or otherwise;
   (b) where the invention is a process, he uses the process or he offers it for use in the UK when he knows, or it is obvious to a reasonable person in the circumstances,

that its use there without the consent of the proprietor would be an infringement of the patent;

(c) where the invention is a process, he disposes of, offers to dispose of, uses or imports any product obtained directly by means of that process or keeps any such product whether for disposal or otherwise.

**2.** Product patents:

Intention is irrelevant – *Proctor v Bennis* (1887). For s60(1)(a), there are a number of rights, and these are as follows:

(i) The 'right to make'.
This might be infringed when modifications or repairs are made to a patented product. In *United Wire v Screen Repair Services* (2000) Lord Hoffman said that purchasers of patented products should be able to repair and modify products. Generally though, a repairer should not repair the 'essential component' or 'essential element' of a product. This remains uncertain as to precise scope.

(ii) The 'right to dispose'.
The right to sell the product.
This does *not* mean that others cannot sell the product at a later date, due to the doctrine of exhaustion. Also note the common law doctrine of implied license.

(iii) The 'Right to import'.
There is a need to be in trade or in making profit to infringe this right. Also note that in *Wilderman* (1925) Tomlin J said:
'I cannot think that the employment of a patented cutting blow pipe or a patented hammer in the manufacture of some part of a locomotive would necessarily render the importation of the locomotive an infringement'.

(iv) The 'right to keep the product'.
This applies when an infringer keeps the product, *for disposal or otherwise*. In *SKF* (1980), it was said that the passive storing of a patented drug in a London BA

warehouse could be contrary to s60(1). It was held not to be because of the passive nature of the act. This implies that courts seem to take a generous view of legitimate activity, even though there is no actual defence of innocence. The *SKF* decision may be contrasted with *McDonald v Graham* (1994), where a marketing consultant made some articles available to a third party without consent. It was beneficial to the marketing consultant.

**3.** Process patents.
- The key section for process patents is s60(1)(b).
- Note that process patents are treated differently to product patents, in that knowledge is required for process patents, and the same is true for product by process patents. However, if knowledge cannot be proved, it can be replaced by the phrase 'or it is obvious to a reasonable person in the circumstances'.
- The party making the offer must know (i.e. have subjective knowledge) or it must be obvious in the circumstances (i.e. an objective standard) that the use of the process would be 'an infringement of the patent'. This appears to require not only knowledge that the use involves applying the inventive concept in question, but also that the inventive concept is patent protected. (Compare to secondary infringement under s60(2).)

**4.** Product by process patents.
- The rights of disposal, to keep and so on bear the same meanings as in s60(1)(a), discussed above.
- Note that a product by process patent must be a direct product of the patented process. This could potentially be construed widely, so the potential scope has been limited. Thus, there should not be any important and material steps intervening in the 'directness' between product and process.
- In *Pioneer v Warner Music* (1997) it was unclear if there was a direct relationship between the process patent and some imported discs. The Court of Appeal said there

should not be an intermediary. In this case, it was held that there were no important or material steps. A step would be only not be included if that step was immaterial or trivial.

### 5.2.2 Secondary infringement

1. There is again the requirement that a secondary infringer should have knowledge, or that the secondary infringer should have had knowledge.
2. According to s60(2), where they supply or offer to supply a means relating to an essential element of the invention for putting the inventions into effect, three elements should be satisfied:

> **(a) the patent proprietor must establish that the means supplied by the defendant relate to an essential element of the invention;**
> **(b) the supplier must know, or should know, that the means are both suitable for and are intended for putting the invention into effect [with objective knowledge];**
> **(c) that there is *not* a legitimate reason for the secondary infringement, namely is it a staple article of commerce.**

3. The staple article of commerce doctrine is found in s60(3). This states:
'S60(3) Subsection (2) above shall not apply to the supply or offer of a staple commercial product unless the supply or the offer is made for the purpose of inducing the person supplied or, as the case may be, the person to whom the offer is made to do an act which constitutes an infringement of the patent by virtue of subsection (1) above.' The 'staple commercial product' requirement means that the product should be a standard product.

## 5.3 CLAIM INTERPRETATION

1. Claim interpretation is important for assessing whether the alleged infringing invention falls within the scope of the

patent claims. The key section is s125(1) Patents Act 1977: 'S125(1) For the purposes of this Act, an invention for a patent for which an application has been made or for which a patent has been granted shall, unless the context otherwise requires, be taken to be that specified in a claim of the specification of the application or patent, as the case may be, as interpreted by the description and any drawing contained in that specification, and the extent of the protection conferred by a patent shall be determined accordingly.'

## 5.3.1 Early law relating to claim interpretation

1. Textual infringement does not often occur. Instead, focus will often be on variants. To deal with this problem the courts once used the 'pith and marrow' doctrine. In *C van der Lely v Bamfords* (1963), Viscount Radcliffe said: 'After all, it is [the patentee] who has committed himself to the unequivocal description of what he claims to have invented, and he must submit in the first place to be judged by his own actions and words.'
2. Although English judges have been more at home with a literal approach, there was dissent. Lord Reid, in *Rodi & Weinenberger v Henry Showell* (1969) wrote: '... claims are not addressed to conveyancers: they are addressed to practical men skilled in the prior art, and I do not think that they ought to be construed with that meticulousness which was once thought appropriate to conveyancing documents.'
(Note that he was not in the majority.)
3. Judges were to study the specification and what the alleged infringer had done.
   - If the defendant's activities fell within the claims, then there was infringement.
   - If there were variations, then the court should have determined whether there were fundamental differences between the patentee's invention and what the alleged infringer had produced.

- In other words, each element or section of the claim (or integers) was to be looked at, followed by consideration of how many integers had been taken by the defendant, and the extent to which those integers were vital to the working of the invention.

## 5.4 THE UNDERPINNINGS OF THE CURRENT APPROACH

1. *Catnic Components v Hill & Smith* (1982) is the first important case to bear in mind. However, from the outset, note that this concerned a claim under the 1949 Patents Act. The effect of the case on the Patents Act 1977 was questioned until its importance was confirmed in *Improver v Remington* (1990). The following are the key points:

**(i) Would a person with practical knowledge and experience understand that strict compliance with a particular descriptive word or phrase appearing in a claim was intended by the patentee to be an essential requirement of the invention so that any variant would fall outside the monopoly claimed, even though it could have no material effect upon the way the invention worked. That question does not arise where the variant would in fact have a material effect upon the way the invention worked.**

↓

**(ii) At the date of publication of the specification was it obvious to the informed reader that this was so?**

↓

**(iii) Where it is not obvious, in the light of the then-existing knowledge, the reader is to assume that the patentee thought at the time of the specification that he had good reason for limiting his monopoly so strictly, unless it is clear otherwise it could have been intended by the patentee.**

## 5.5 The approach since the Protocol

1. With claim interpretation, it is now important to note the Protocol on the Interpretation of Article 69 EPC. In the Patents Act 1977, s125(3) states:
   'The Protocol on the Interpretation of Article 69 of the European Patent Convention (which Article contains a provision corresponding to subsection (1) above) shall, as for the time being in force, apply for the purposes of subsection (1) above as it applies for the purposes of that Article.'
2. The Protocol on the Interpretation of Article 69 EPC states:
   'Article 69 should not be interpreted in the sense that the extent of the protection conferred by a European patent is to be understood as that defined by the strict, literal, meaning of the wording used in the claims, the description and drawings being employed only for the purpose of resolving ambiguity found in the claims. Neither should it be interpreted in the sense that the claims serve only as a guideline and that the actual protection conferred may extend to what, from a consideration of the description by a person skilled in the art, the patentee has contemplated. On the contrary, it is to be interpreted as defining a position between these extremes which combines a fair protection for the patentee with a reasonable degree of certainty for third parties.'
3. The current method of applying the Protocol is shown in *Improver v Remington* (1990), which has a set of questions known as the 'Protocol Questions':

- **Does the variant have a material effect on the way the invention works? If no, proceed to the next question.**
- **Would this have been obvious to the person skilled in the art at the time of the publication? (Note that other countries often say at the time of the infringement.) If yes, then proceed to ask:**
- **Would the reader skilled in the art have nevertheless realised strict compliance with the intended meaning was an essential requirement of the invention? (If no, then this indicates an infringement has taken place.)**

4. According to Lord Hoffman, construction of claims is dealt with in the third part.
5. However, there was a degree of uncertainty for a time over application of the test.
   - In *PLG v Ardon* (1995) it was stated that one should ask whether the variant embodied in the disputed device was one which was deducible by a person skilled in the art from the wording and drawings of the claims. Thus it was not asked whether the wording of the claims revealed that the patentee intended strict compliance with a particular feature.
   - Furthermore, *Daily v Berchet* (1992) went though variant after variant, which was more akin to going back to the pith and marrow approach.
6. Recent guidance as to the Protocol Questions were, however, given by Lord Hoffman in *Kirin Amgen* (2005).
   - He clarified that the pith and marrow doctrine was expressly prohibited by the Protocol, and that the interpretation of Art 69 EPC governs the applicable rules for the construction of patents under Art 69, not the construction of individual claims (therefore sidelining the arguments of the Court of Appeal in *PLG*).
   - However, he did stress that the Protocol Questions should only be considered as guidelines, and furthermore, that the Protocol Questions may be unhelpful in the case of new technologies.
   - As such, although clarifying the applicability of the Protocol Questions, *Kirin Amgen* still leaves uncertainty as to when, in practice, the questions will be applied.

## 5.6 DEFENCES

1. The purpose of defence to patent infringement may be said to remedy market defects. The defences are mostly contained within s60(5) [derived from Art 27 CPC]. There are, however, some other important sections, namely s74(1)(g) and s64(1).

### 5.6.1 S74(1)(g)

1. Under s74(1)(g), the validity of a patent may be put in issue by way of defence to proceedings for infringement. Where a defendant attempts to demonstrate that the infringing activity was being carried out in public before the priority date of the patent, it is possible to force the patentee to either:
   (a) require that the patent be interpreted so as to exclude the activity; or
   (b) accept that the patent covers the activity and is therefore invalid (e.g. for want of novelty).

### 5.6.2 S64(1)

1. The other important section is s64(1), which concerns prior use. This states:
   'S64 Right to continue use begun before priority date:
   (1) Where a patent is granted for an invention, a person who in the United Kingdom before the priority date of the invention:
      (a) does in good faith an act which would constitute an infringement of the patent if it were in force, or
      (b) makes in good faith effective and serious preparations to do such an act,
   has the right to continue to do the act or, as the case may be, to do the act, notwithstanding the grant of the patent; but this right does not extend to granting a licence to another person to do the act.'
2. The section is a personal defence, which means that the secret use must be by the same person or partner. Note the section only applies to acts done within the UK for the purposes of the statute.
3. In relation to s64(1)(b), note the phrase 'effective and serious preparations'. These have been said to mean that the use 'must be so advanced as to be about to result in the

infringing act': *Lubrizol v Esso Petroleum Ltd* (1998). There should also be a clear link of causation between the prior use and the infringing use.

## 5.7 DEFENCES UNDER S60(5)

1. In relation to the defences enshrined within s60(5), these are as follows:
2. S60(5)(a):
   This concerns acts done privately for non commercial uses. These are not a threat to the patent monopoly. They need not be secret or confidential, but they must be the person's own use. If there are both commercial and private aspects, then the court looks at the subjective intention of the user.
3. S60(5)(b):
   This provides immunity for acts done for experimental purposes relating to the subject matter of the invention.
   - The reasoning is that a monopoly should not be allowed to inhibit scientific developments.
   - A valid experimental purpose is to discover something unknown or to test a hypothesis. This may be to discover if an invention actually works.
   - Likewise, it could be applicable where a party is thinking to license a patent or be a licensee – or if they believe a patent is invalid on grounds of insufficiency.
   - However, the exception will not apply if the purpose is to prove something already known, or to demonstrate a product works in the way claimed, or to obtain official approval.
   - Generally, if there is a commercial reason behind the experiment, it will not be caught by s60(5)(b). This may have repercussions in the field of biotechnology.
4. S60(5)(c):
   This is a defence for an infringement which consists of the extemporaneous preparation in a pharmacy of a medicine for an individual in accordance with a prescription given by

a registered medical or dental practitioner or consists of dealing with a medicine so prepared. It is, in other words, rather narrow.

5. S60(5)(d)-(f)
   These sections concern infringement caused by travelling into jurisdictions where a patent is protected. The sections are as follows:
   'An act which, apart from this subsection, would constitute an infringement of a patent for an invention shall not do so if:
   ...
   (d) it consists of the use, exclusively for the needs of a relevant ship, of a product or process in the body of such a ship or in its machinery, tackle, apparatus or other accessories, in a case where the ship has temporarily or accidentally entered the internal or territorial waters of the United Kingdom;
   (e) it consists of the use of a product or process in the body or operation of a relevant aircraft, hovercraft or vehicle which has temporarily or accidentally entered or is crossing the United Kingdom (including the air space above it and its territorial waters) or the use of accessories for such a relevant aircraft, hovercraft or vehicle;
   (f) it consists of the use of an exempted aircraft which has lawfully entered or is lawfully crossing the United Kingdom as aforesaid or of the importation into the United Kingdom, or the use or storage there, of any part or accessory for such an aircraft ...'
6. S60(5)(g)-(h) Farmers Privilege (from the Biotechnology Directive).
   'An act which, apart from this subsection, would constitute an infringement of a patent for an invention shall not do so if:
   ...
   (g) it consists of the use by a farmer of the product of his harvest for propagation or multiplication by him on

his own holding, where there has been a sale of plant propagating material to the farmer by the proprietor of the patent or with his consent for agricultural use;

(h) it consists of the use of an animal or animal reproductive material by a farmer for an agricultural purpose following a sale to the farmer, by the proprietor of the patent or with his consent, of breeding stock or other animal reproductive material which constitutes or contains the patented invention.'

**7.** You should note Art 10 of the Biotechnology Directive. This states that protection:
'shall not extend to biological material obtained from the propagation or multiplication of biological material placed on the market by the owner of the patent where the multiplication or propagation necessarily results from the application for which the biological material was marketed.'
Thus, said to be the *necessary* incident of the true purpose of sale.

**8.** The seed sowing privilege in s60(5)(g) is to enable farmers to save seed from *one* year's crop to sow them the following year. Note s60(5)(g) applies to a list of plants contained within Schedule A1 paragraph 2. S60(5)(h) is a similar provision for animals, although it is potentially very broad. This applies primarily within the context of genetically modified animals. Thus, a farmer may breed his own animals even though they contain genetically modified matter. Note the defence does not include sale or other commercial activity.

CHAPTER 6

# UK REGISTERED TRADEMARKS – ABSOLUTE GROUNDS FOR REFUSA

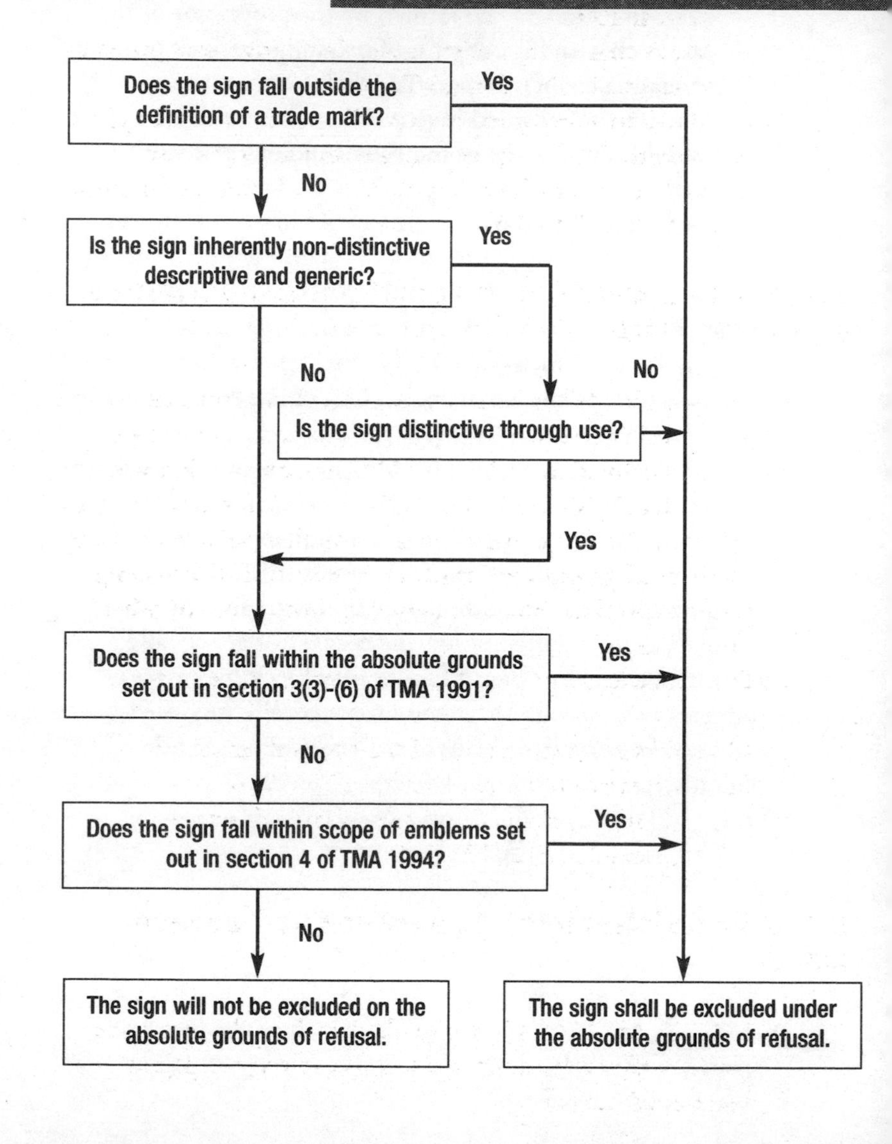

Does the sign fall outside the definition of a trade mark?
Yes
No
Is the sign inherently non-distinctive descriptive and generic?
Yes
No
No
Is the sign distinctive through use?
Yes
Does the sign fall within the absolute grounds set out in section 3(3)-(6) of TMA 1991?
Yes
No
Does the sign fall within scope of emblems set out in section 4 of TMA 1994?
Yes
No
The sign will not be excluded on the absolute grounds of refusal.
The sign shall be excluded under the absolute grounds of refusal.

# 6.1 INTRODUCTION

1. There are three main groups for absolute grounds of refusal:
   - Signs that fall outside of the statutory definition of a trade mark under s3(1)(a) and s3(2) Trade Marks Act (TMA) 1994.
   - Marks that are non-distinctive, descriptive, and general as set out in s3(1)(b)–(d) TMA 1994.
   - Marks that are contrary to public policy or morality; are likely to deceive the public; are prohibited by law; or application of which was made in bad faith, as set out in s3(3)–(6) TMA 1994.

## 6.1.1 A sign which falls outside of the definition of a trade mark

1. A sign which falls outside of the definition of a trade mark is a sign which does not satisfy the requirements of a trade mark as defined in s1(1)(a) TMA 1994. Such a sign will not be registrable (s3(1)(a) TMA 1994). S1(1)(a) states: 'S1(1)(a) ... a "trade mark" means any sign capable of being represented graphically which is capable of distinguishing goods or services of one undertaking from those of other undertakings.'
2. Furthermore, a sign which consists exclusively of a shape which:
   (i) results from the nature of the goods themselves;
   (ii) is necessary to obtain a technical result; or
   (iii) gives substantial value to the goods, will not be registerable (s3(2) TMA 1994).

## 6.1.2 Non-distinctive, descriptive and generic marks

1. S3(1)(b)–(d) TMA 1994 provide that the following trade marks shall not be registered (subject to the exceptions mentioned below):

'S3(1)(b) trade marks which are devoid of any distinctive character;
S3(1)(c) trade marks which consist exclusively of signs or indications which may serve, in trade, to designate the kind, quality, quantity, intended purpose, value, geographical origin, or the time of production of the goods or of the rendering of the service, or other characteristics of the goods or service;
S3(1)(d) trade marks which consist exclusively of signs or indications which have become customary in the current language or in the *bona fide* and established practises of the trade.'

2. The rationale behind the absolute grounds set out in s3(1)(b)–(d) are to ensure:
   - that consumers can distinguish between the signs and the goods and/or services of rival traders; and
   - to minimise any negative impact that the grant of trade marks may have upon traders working in the same or related areas.
3. In considering whether a trade mark *inherently* falls within the scope of s3(1)(b)–(d), the tribunals and the courts will assess the *distinctiveness* of the trade mark in question using the following tests:
   (a) The impact that monopolisation of that sign would have on other traders (Lord Parker's test in *W & G Du Cross' Application* (1913)).
   (b) Whether the sign will be perceived by a relevant consumer as an indication that goods or services come from a single geographical source, e.g. whether the geographical name is capable, in the mind of the relevant class of persons, of designating the origin of the category of the goods in question (per the ECJ in *Windsurfing Chiemsee v Attenberger* (1999)).
   (c) If the sign is a purely descriptive one, then the prohibition on registration is because they can no longer fulfil the purpose of identifying the undertaking marketing them and are therefore devoid of distinctive

character (per the ECJ in *Proctor & Gamble Co v OHIM (Baby Dry)* (2002)).

(d) If the sign is descriptive or could be used for descriptive purposes, then it should be excluded from registration if at least one of its possible meanings designates a characteristic of the goods or services concerned. This is based on the idea of whether a sign is capable of being used by other traders to designate a characteristic of their goods or services.

**4.** In applying the above tests, the courts held the view that:

(a) the assessment would involve a combination of objective and subjective elements and that the examiner would enjoy a certain degree of discretion;

(b) the relevant consumers would be those 'reasonably well-informed and reasonably observant and circumspect' (*Bach Flower Remedies v Healing Herbs* (2000)).

### 6.1.3 Signs devoid of distinctive character

**1.** In what circumstances may a sign be held to be devoid of distinctive character and therefore excluded under s3(1)(b) TMA 1994?

**2.** Letters, numbers and grammatical signs:

- In most cases single letters, numbers, and grammatical signs will be treated as 'devoid of distinctive character'.
- The scope of the exclusion under s3(1)(b)–(d) TMA 1994 is beyond a literal reading of the sign to include obvious and immaterial variations, as well as variants common in trade, for example, adding hyphens or exclamation marks, the omission of grammatical features, the addition of commonplace borders or motif, being used in an ungrammatical way and combining, shortening or telescoping two or more unregistrable terms.
- A word that is phonetically equivalent to an unregistrable word will usually be unregistrable.
- A word that is the foreign equivalence of an unregistrable word is unlikely be registerable. The test

takes into account the extent to which the mark is recognised in its original language, how widely the language is spoken in the UK, how familiar the word is, and how common it is for the foreign word to be used in that trade. In consideration of the combinations of letters and numbers, abbreviations or initials, the following factors will be taken into account:

(i) length of the series of initials;
(ii) the way the combination would be pronounced;
(iii) whether they are presented as initials;
(iv) whether numbers, letters and the dates might be taken to indicate catalogue numbers, sizes, model numbers, date of productions, etc.

**3.** Pictorial marks:
- A single line, square, or colour will usually be devoid of distinctive character.
- The mixed device marks with words which are not themselves registrable will usually be devoid of distinctive character.

**4.** Colour marks:
- Complex colour combinations or patterns are more likely to be distinctive compared to simple colours. Note that the ECJ has noted that there is a strong public interest in keeping colours free (*Libertel Groep BGV v Benelux-Merkenbureau* (2004)).
- A colour would only be distinctive, in the absence of use, where it was a shade which is extremely unusual and peculiar in the relevant trade or whether it is to be used for very specific goods for very specific clients.

**5.** Shape marks:
- A functional shape is likely to be treated as inherently non-distinctive.
- An assessment of whether the shape is registerable requires first an assessment as to whether there is anything unusual or idiosyncratic about the shape such that the relevant consumer would remember it; followed by an assessment whether the consumer would think of

the shape as being indicative of source rather than being merely functional or decorative.

- It might also be necessary to consider whether the shape is one which needs to be left in the public domain.

**6.** Packaging:

- In most cases the packaging of a product will be non-distinctive as average customers do not treat the majority of packaging as indicating source, but rather the literature on packaging.
- If the difference in the outward appearance and packaging of the same products become apparent only on close examination and comparison, neither can be said to be distinctive.
- Where the sign is capable of creating in the minds of consumers the necessary link between the products and a particular trader, the shape mark can be distinctive. Following *Nestlé Waters France v OHIM (Bottle Shape)* (2004), the key element could be whether traders have educated consumers to view the packaging as indicative of commercial origin. Thus if packaging is devoid of distinctive character, it will depend on the circumstances as to whether it will catch the attention of consumers.

**7.** Names and signatures:

- Common forenames or surnames are unlikely to be distinctive as consumers are unable to assume that the name operates to indicate one particular supplier. Whether names in questions are famous is not relevant. (See, e.g., *Elvis Presley Trade Marks* (1999).)
- The types of goods or services for which registration was sought are one of the factors to be taken into account in deciding whether a name is distinctive, e.g. for solicitors or coach companies, the common surnames will not be distinctive.
- Signatures are generally treated as distinctive even if it is not written in a distinctive graphic style or not even authentic.

## 6.2 DESCRIPTIVE MARKS WHICH EXCLUSIVELY CONSIST OF CERTAIN SIGNS AND INDICATIONS

### 6.2.1 Definition of exclusively

1. Is the sign in question a *descriptive* mark which *exclusively* consists of certain signs and indications? If it is, it will be excluded under s3(1)(c) TMA 1994.
2. What is meant by the word 'exclusively'?
   - For s3(1)(c) TMA 1994 purposes, the whole of a mark must be descriptive.
   - If part of a mark is non-descriptive, it will not be an exclusively descriptive mark. The additional non-descriptive element must be fanciful, imaginative, unusual or peculiar.
   - A descriptive mark will not be wholly descriptive if it is applied to unrelated products in a fanciful way and is affected by some alteration which is:
     (i) sufficiently distinctive; or
     (ii) combined with other descriptive signs to result in a new single word without an obvious meaning or understandable reference to specific goods or services.
   - A word with double meaning will not be exclusively descriptive if an average consumer would understand the sign *immediately and without further thought as bearing a single meaning* that describes the goods or services.

### 6.2.2 Categories excluded by s3(1)(c) TMA 1994

1. The following categories of descriptive marks are excluded by s3(1)(c) TMA 1994.
2. 'Kind, quality or quantity' of goods and/or services:

- The sign will fall within this group if it has direct reference to the kind, quality or quantity of the goods or services.
- There is no statutory definition for 'kind, quality and quantity'.
- Whether a word has direct reference to 'kind, quality or quantity' of products and services will depend on the nature of the products and services.
- Longevity or treatment could be relevant to the quality of certain products such as perfume or desert sauces (e.g. *British Sugar v James Robertson & Sons* (1996)).

**3.** Intended purpose:

- A mark which describes:
  - (i) what a product or service does;
  - (ii) what the consumer is to do with a product or service; or
  - (iii) what happens after the consumption of a product or service will be a description of 'intended purposes' of products or service.
- A mark which describes only one of the intended purposes of a product or service will still be excluded under s3(1)(c) TMA 1994.
- The intended purposes shall be decided from the point of view of average customers.

**4.** Value:

- A word such as 'pound' is not completely excluded unless it is used in a way which is common for describing the value of a product or service.

**5.** Geographical origin:

- The names of geographical origin have traditionally meant those references to continents, countries, cities, towns, rivers, and occasionally even streets.
- However, there is not a total ban on the registration of all geographical names.
- For s3(1)(c) TMA 1994 to apply to a geographical origin, there must be a connection between the place

and products or services of the sort in question (*Windsurfing Chiemsee v Attenberger* (1999)).
   - The connection can be a *belief* that the goods were manufactured, conceived or designed in a particular place in question.
   - Based on the established connection, the examiner will assess the likelihood of other traders coming to trade in the place in question. The larger the place, the more likely other traders will want to use it, the more likely the place will be excluded under s3(1)(c) TMA 1994.
6. The time of production of the goods or the time of rendering of the services:
   - This may exclude marks which reference to centuries, decades, years, seasons, public holidays and days of the week.
7. Other characteristics:
   - This is a catch-all provision.
   - It can easily catch characteristics such as flavour, shape, colour and packaging which have not been specified in the above provisions.

## 6.3 IS THE SIGN IN QUESTION AN *EXCLUSIVELY CUSTOMARY AND GENERIC* MARK WHICH WILL BE EXCLUDED UNDER S3(1)(D)?

### 6.3.1 Exclusively

1. What is meant by 'exclusively'?
   - It is logical to expect that 'exclusively' will bear a similar meaning as it has in s3(1)(c).

### 6.3.2 Generic marks

1. Generic marks:
   - One of the features of a generic mark is that it is incapable of distinguishing the goods or services of different traders.
   - A name of a product or service is usually a generic mark.

### 6.3.3 Customary pictures

1. The definition of customary pictures is:
   - A picture which is made up of a conventional representation of the category or type of products or a scene widely associated with its production.
   - For example, a picture of grapes and vine leaves for wine, flowers for perfume, and cats and dogs for pet food.

### 6.3.4 Distinctive marks

1. Evidence about other marks on the Register is in principle irrelevant when considering a trade mark tendered for registration, subject to the exception for a mark that is being added to a family of marks.
2. However, s3(1)(b)–(d) TMA 1994 are subject to a proviso in s3 that a sign which falls within any of the above sub-sections is not to be treated as invalid if it has, as a result of use, 'acquired distinctive character'.
3. A mark which is inherently lacking of distinctiveness can be registered or remained as a trade mark if it becomes 'in fact' distinctive. There are two requirements to be 'in fact' distinctive:
   (i) the mark in question must have been used; and
   (ii) the mark has in fact acquired a distinctive character.

4. The test for 'distinctive character' through use is customer recognition, i.e. the primary significance of the word or sign indicates a source rather than merely decrypting or praising the product or service. The sign carries 'secondary meaning'.
5. A sign can be distinctive even if the secondary meaning does not displace its primary meaning completely. However, displacement of primary meaning may be required when the sign is used with certain particular goods or services. In such a case, the test will be whether the average customer immediately understands the sign as referring to source.
6. Any ambiguity in relation to the meanings of the sign will be treated as devoid of distinctive character.
7. The burden of proof is on the applicant to prove the 'acquired distinctiveness'.
8. The more descriptive a mark is, the more convincing must be the evidence of acquired distinctiveness, and the more extent of recognition from the relevant customers is required. This is a question of degree.
9. The following factors shall be taken into account in deciding whether the distinctiveness through use has been established:
   - Market share held by the mark.
   - How intensive, geographically widespread and longstanding use of the mark is.
   - Amount invested in promoting the mark.
   - The proportion of the relevant customers who identify goods as originating from a particular trader because of the mark.
   - Statements from chambers of commerce and industry or other trade and professional associations.

### 6.3.5 Registrable marks

1. Where a sign is used as an advertising slogan, it is unlikely that it will transform an inherently unregistrable mark into one that is registrable. For an advertising slogan to be registrable, it has to be shown by evidence of some branding function.

2. Where a name or image is primarily used for ornamental or decorative purposes, it is unlikely that it will be registrable.
3. For a mark used in combination with other marks to be registrable, it must be shown that the mark in question, among the other marks, is the one which is mostly associated by relevant customers with a product or service.
4. The evidence of advertising expenditure and use will not definitely lead to a finding of distinctiveness through use.
5. Direct evidence from consumer surveys will most likely be of value in deciding distinctiveness through use.

## 6.4 Other Absolute Grounds of Refusal

1. S3(3)–(6) TMA 1994 provides that the marks shall not be registered if they are contrary to:
   - public policy or morality;
   - likely to deceive the public;
   - are prohibited by law; or
   - if the application was made in bad faith.
2. S4 TMA 1994 also set out special provisions for protecting certain emblems.

### 6.4.1 Public policy or morality

1. When looking at public policy or morality, the following points should be noted:
   - S3(3)(a) TMA 1994 provides that a trade mark shall not be registered if it is contrary to public policy or to accepted principles of morality.
   - Public policy is confined to morality, and does not include economic concerns.
   - A mark which is likely to cause confusion between two products can be excluded on the ground of public policy.
   - A registration of a mark which might be believed by the public as a form of official sanction or approval can be excluded on the ground of public policy.

- It may be difficult to draw the line between marks which contravene principles of morality and those that are simply in poor taste. However, the marks will only be excluded under the public policy ground where they offend the generally accepted mores of the time.

### 6.4.2 Marks which could deceive the public

1. Deceptive marks:
   - S3(3)(b) TMA 1994 provides that a trade mark shall not be registered if it is 'of such a nature as to deceive the public' (e.g. as to the nature of the goods).
   - Marks which, though distinctive, contain some kind of suggestion or allusion that is inaccurate will be excluded under s3(3)(b) TMA 1994.
   - If the misdescription is obvious and is such that it would immediately be corrected by further observations by consumers, such misdescriptions will not render marks excluded under s3(3)(b).
   - If a mark gives rise to a real but inaccurate expectation that the goods are from a particular locality, it can be excluded under s3(3)(b).

### 6.4.3 Prohibited marks

1. Marks prohibited by law:
   - S3(4) TMA 1994 provides that a trade mark shall not be registered if its use is prohibited in the United Kingdom, by any enactment or rule of law or by any provision of Community law.
   - The illegality must be intrinsic or inherently in the mark, rather than in the goods for which its use is proposed.
   - The illegality prevents the registration of 'protected designations of origin' and 'geographical indication' for wines, spirits, agricultural products and food.

### 6.4.4 Bad faith

1. Application in bad faith:
   S3(6) TMA 1994 provides that a trade mark shall not be registered if, or to the extent that the application is made, in bad faith.
2. There is no clear definition for 'bad faith'.
3. The following situations may constitute 'bad faith' in giving its literal meaning:
   - No intention to use the mark.
   - Knowledge of third party claims.
   - Use of names or image of well-known person without their consent.
4. A mark may be excluded as the applicant had made the application without genuine intention of using the mark in trade.
5. Lack of intent can be found where:
   - A person applies to register a mark with the intent either of preventing a competitor registering the mark or selling the registered right.
   - A person applies to register a mark that is similar to an unregistrable mark which the trader is in fact using (a ghost mark).
   - A person applies to register a mark at a time when they are clearly unable to use that mark for the goods or services in question.
   - A person applies to register a mark to the goods or services, of which the specification is unduly broad.
6. The applicant may be held to lack good faith if the applicant is aware of a third party intending to register a mark. This can be found where:
   - There is a breach of trust between the applicant and the third party, whether or not the application constitutes a breach of a legal obligation, e.g. where the applicant is an employee or an agent of the third party.

- An applicant copies a mark being used aboard with the intention of pre-empting the foreign user who intends to trade in the United Kingdom.

### 6.4.5 Specially protected emblems

**1.** Special emblems:
- S4 TMA 1994 provides that trade marks shall not be registered if they consist of specially protected emblems.
- The specially protected emblems include:
  - (i) various signs in connection with the Crown, such as the Royal arms, the Royal crown and flags, any representation of any member of the Royal family or any other sign suggesting that the applicant has Royal patronage;
  - (ii) various national and international emblems and flags;
  - (iii) coats of arms;
  - (iv) the emblems and flags for other Convention countries as listed in ss57 and 58 TMA 1994.

# CHAPTER 7

# RELATIVE GROUNDS FOR REFUSAL OF A TRADEMARK

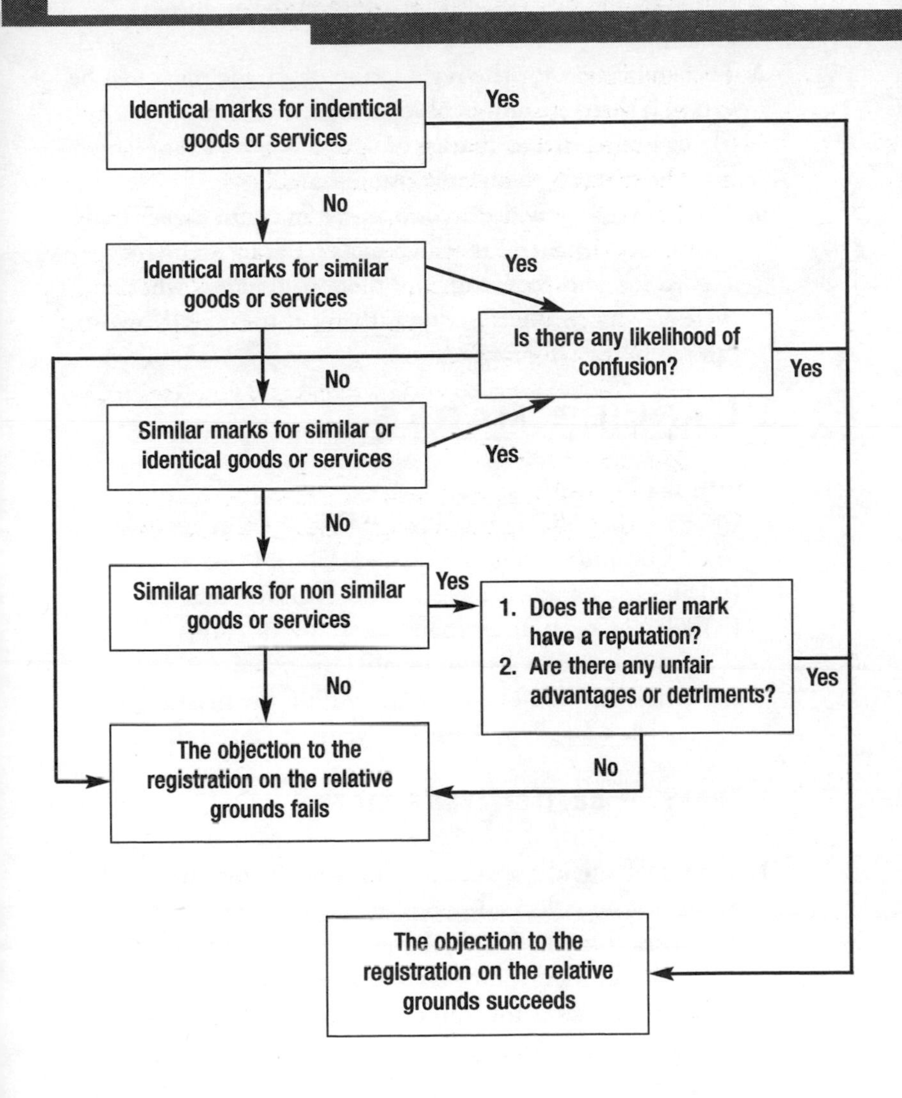

## 7.1 INTRODUCTION

1. The relative grounds are the grounds on which the application of the registration of the trademark can be barred by the UK Registry in addition to the absolute grounds.
2. The application for the registration of a trade mark can be barred if there are any conflicts with:
   (i) earlier registered marks; or
   (ii) earlier rights to an unregistered mark.
3. The UK registry will *ex officio* search for both earlier trade marks and earlier rights which are similar to the mark applied for, and then compare them to find out whether there are any conflicts between them. If so, the UK registry can refuse the later application.

## 7.2 EARLIER MARKS

1. 'Earlier marks' includes:
   (i) an earlier UK or international registration (s6(1)(a));
   (ii) a Community registration (s6(1)(a));
   (iii) an earlier application any of the above (s6(2));
   (iv) a later Community mark based on the earlier UK or international registration (s6(1)(b)); and
   (v) an earlier 'well-known' mark within the meaning of Article 6*bis* of the Paris Convention (s6(1)(c)).

### 7.2.1 Types of earlier trade marks

1. TMA 1994 divides the earlier trade marks into three types:
   - identical marks and goods or service (s5(1));
   - identical marks for similar goods or service *or* similar marks for identical or similar goods or services (s5(2));
   - identical marks for non-similar goods or services (s5(3)).

### 7.2.2 Identical marks for identical goods or services

1. In accordance with s5(1), both the marks being compared and the goods or services for which the marks are used are identical. The confusion of the identity of marks and goods or services is assumed.
2. Identical sign requires an examination of what actually appears on the register – see *Philips Electronics NV v Remington Consumer Products* (1998). If the registered mark consists of a word, the typeface or style of lettering is irrelevant (*Bravado Merchandising v Mainstream Publishing* (1996)).
3. The ECJ has held that the test for the identical sign is that a sign is identical with the earlier trade mark where it produces, without any modification or addition, all the elements constituting the trade mark or where, viewed as a whole, it contains differences so insignificant that they may go unnoticed by an average consumer (*LTJ Diffusion SA v Sadas Vertbaudet SA* (2003)).
4. Two marks will be 'identical' where:
   (i) there is only minimis difference between two marks, for example 'Origin' and 'Origins'; or
   (ii) part of the mark is identical and both of the marks are used with associated matters. For example, the mark 'Robertson's Toffee Treat' was deemed identical to the mark 'Treat' used with the well-known mark 'Silver Spoon' (*British Sugar v James Robertson* (1996)).

### 7.2.3 Identical marks for similar goods or services

1. Similar marks for identical or similar goods or services *or* identical marks for similar goods or services.
2. The application for the registration of a trade mark may be barred if:

(i) the identical marks are used on the similar goods or services; or

(ii) the similar marks are used on the identical or similar goods or services, provided a likelihood of confusion on the part of public must be shown (s5(2)).

3. The test for the similarities of marks is the visual and conceptual and aural similarities based on the overall impression given by the marks bearing in mind their distinctive components (*Sabel BV v Puma AG* (1997)).
4. In considering of the similarities of goods or services, all relevant factors have to be taken into account, including:
   - the nature of goods or services;
   - the end users;
   - the method of use;
   - where they are in competition with each other or are complementary.
5. The confusion shall include the likelihood of associating later goods and services with the earlier trade mark by the public.
6. The types of confusion may include:
   - direct (confusing the products);
   - indirect (thinking that the goods come from economically linked undertakings or that the trade mark owner has expanded their product line);
   - mere calling to mind.
7. It is for the trade mark office or national court to assess the likelihood of confusion, taking into account all factors relevant to the circumstances of the case.
8. The test is whether there is a genuine and properly substantiated likelihood of confusion on the part of an average consumer. A mere calling to mind will not be sufficient for finding a substantiated likelihood of confusion.
9. An average consumer shall be a person who is reasonably well informed and reasonably observant and circumspect.
10. Accounts have to be given that the average consumer's level of attention will vary for different types of goods and services.

**11.** Recital 10 of the Directive states that:
'Whereas it is indispensable to give an interpretation of the concept of similarity in relation to the likelihood of confusion, the appreciation of which depends on numerous elements and, in particular, on the recognition of the trade mark on the market, of the association which can be made with the used or registered sign, of the degree of similarity between the trademark and the sign and between the goods or services identified …'

**12.** The more distinctive the prior mark has become through use, the more probable that there will be confusion.

**13.** It is held in *Canon KK v Metro-Goldwyn-Mayer Inc* (1998) that:
'A global assessment of the likelihood of confusion implies some interdependence between the relevant factors, and in particular a similarity between the trade marks and between these goods or services.'

**14.** The strength of the earlier trade mark may have the effect of making dissimilar goods similar, or the closeness of the goods may make the sign more similar to the earlier mark.

### 7.2.4 Similar or identical marks for non-similar goods or services

**1.** A relative ground for barring the application for a trade mark registration exists if:
   (i) an earlier similar mark for non-similar goods or services has a reputation in the UK; and
   (ii) the use of the later trade mark without due cause would take unfair advantage of, or be detrimental to, the distinctive character or repute of the earlier trade mark (s5(3)).

**2.** The reputation does not mean 'well-known' or 'famous'. However, the owner of the earlier mark has to be able to prove a substantial degree of recognition.

3. It was held in *General Motors Corporation v Yplon SA* (1999) that:
   'The degree of knowledge required must be considered to be reached when the earlier mark is known by a significant part of the public concerned by the products or services covered by that trade mark.'
4. The reputation only need exist in part of the geographical area for which the registration pertains.
5. Notwithstanding the above, confusion by an average consumer will usually be required for such a case. There should be sufficient confusion to lead the public to believe that the owner of the mark with a reputation is extending its line of business. However, the ECJ has held in *Davidoff v Gofked* that the protection must be given to marks with a reputation against use of a sign on similar goods or services even if there is no likelihood of confusion, provided that unfair advantage is taken or detriment is caused to the owner of the earlier mark.
6. The advantages for the later trade mark owner to use the later trade mark must be unfair. It is not intended to enable an owner of the earlier trade mark with a trading reputation to acquire a monopoly on the mark for all trading uses.
7. S5(3) does not intend to have the sweeping effect of preventing the registration of any mark which is the same as, or similar to, a trade mark with a reputation. It is a matter of degree depending on the following factors:
   - The inherent distinctiveness of the earlier trade mark.
   - The extent of reputation which it enjoys.
   - The range of goods or services for which the earlier mark enjoys a reputation.
   - The uniqueness or otherwise of the mark in the market place.
   - Whether the respective goods or services, though dissimilar, are in some way related or likely to be sold through the same outlets.
   - Whether the earlier mark will be any less distinctive than it was before.

- Whether the reputation of the earlier mark is likely to be damaged or tarnished in some significant or material way.

8. The owner of the later trade mark must not have an intention to seek to take advantage of any association which might exist with the earlier mark. However, the advantage must be of a sufficiently significant degree.

## 7.3 Earlier Rights

### 7.3.1 Types of earlier rights

1. There are two types of earlier rights which are qualified for the objections:
   (i) rights to the unregistered trade mark under the passing off laws (s5(4)(a));
   (ii) an earlier copyright, registered design or unregistered design right (s5(4)(b)).

### 7.3.2 Rights to the unregistered trade mark under the passing off laws

1. The use of the mark applied for in the UK will be precluded by any rule of law protecting an unregistered trade mark and other sign used in the course of trade. Passing off laws protect such unregistered trade marks as long as the following three requirements are satisfied, that there is:
   - a protectable reputation in the UK; and
   - a relevant misrepresentation; and
   - the likelihood of damages.

### 7.3.3 Earlier copyright, registered design or unregistered design right

1. For a mark with a reputation, an earlier right can be found if:
   (i) there exists a trading reputation of the earlier trade mark in the UK; and

(ii) the owner of the later trade mark is taking unfair advantage of or causing detriments to the repute of the earlier trade mark.

2. For a well-known mark, an earlier right can be found if the owner can show there is sufficient goodwill in the UK to establish a right to prevent passing off.

## 7.4 Exception to s5: Honest Current Use

1. The UK Registrar has discretion to register a mark which posed some probability of confusion with an earlier registered mark, if the applicant could make out a sufficient case of 'honest concurrent use'.
2. Honest concurrent use is applicable in proceedings between applicant and Registrar before publication.
3. It is necessary to consider:
   - the degree of likely confusion;
   - the honesty of the original adoption and subsequent use of the mark;
   - the length of the applicant's use;
   - evidence of confusion in actual use;
   - the comparative size of trade in the two marks.
4. A period of five years' concurrent use is usually required.

## 7.5 Consent of the Other Party

1. If the owner of the earlier trademarks or earlier rights has given the consent to the registration, the objection falls. The issue of the 'public interest' cannot be raised as one of the grounds for objection.

## 7.6 OBJECTION

1. The objection will only arise where there is indeed an actual right to protect. It is for the Registry or an opponent to prove the grounds for objection.

## 7.7 DISCLAIMER

1. The UK Registry cannot impose the disclaimer of exclusive right in some part of the whole registering marks. However, the applicant can volunteer them to the Registry if there is any doubt on the earlier trade marks or earlier rights.

# CHAPTER 8
# TRADEMARK INFRINGEMENT, REVOCATION AND INVALIDITY

I: Infringement

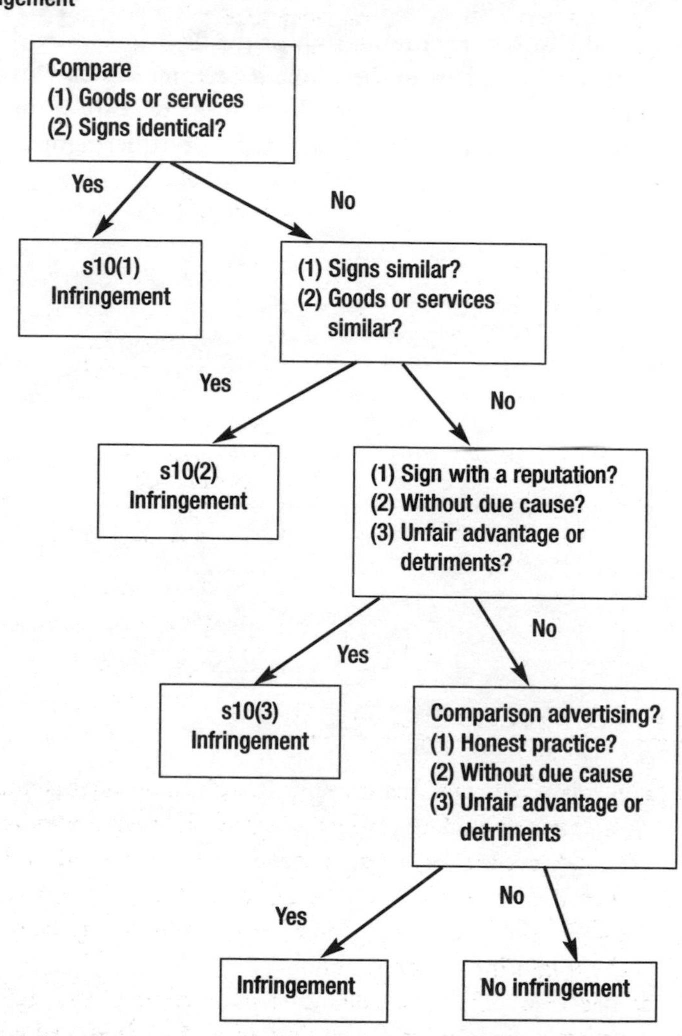

II. Defences

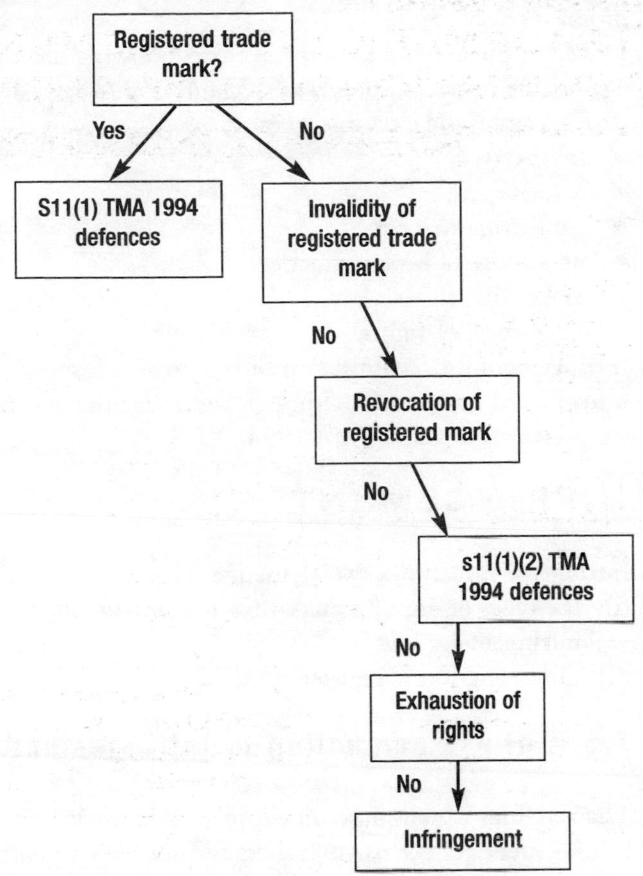


# 8.1 INTRODUCTION

1. A registered trade mark owner can claim an infringement against a defendant using the registered mark or similar sign to indicate the source of its goods or services in accordance with the TMA 1994. However, the TMA 1994 seeks to protect the values in registered marks which may be beyond the origin indication function.
2. The TMA 1994 prohibits three main types of infringing activities in relation to the similarity of signs and of goods

and services, which have a direct correlation to the relative grounds of objection.

3. However, the defendant may have the following defences against the registered proprietor's claim of infringement depending on the circumstances of cases:
   - invalidity;
   - revocation;
   - conflicting marks;
   - unauthorised honest practice;
   - earlier rights;
   - exhaustion of rights.
4. Infringement proceedings cannot be brought for unregistered trademarks, although rights against passing off are preserved in s2(2) TMA 1994.

## 8.2 INFRINGEMENT

1. Infringement includes two elements:
   (i) the types of use of a mark that amounts to an infringement; and
   (ii) the wrong to the registered mark.

### 8.2.1 Types of use amounting to infringement

1. The activities which may constitute a trade mark infringement are extensive. It includes not only a graphic representation of the trade mark but also renditions of the trade mark through sound and smell.
2. Typical infringement involves the use of a sign.

### 8.2.2 The use of a sign

1. The following activities amount to use of a sign under s10(4) TMA 1994 :
   - affixing a sign to goods or packaging;
   - trading in goods or service under a sign;

- importing and exporting goods under a sign;
- using a sign on its business papers or in advertising.

2. An Internet domain name which consists of or contains another's registered mark does not *per se* amount to an infringement. However, the use of the domain name in advertising or a business document or references on the Internet itself is capable of infringing the registered mark (*British Telecom v One in a Million* (1999)).
3. There are three types of use which are defined by TMA 1994 as infringing activities:
   (i) An identical sign for identical goods or services (s10(1)).
   (ii) A similar sign for identical or similar goods or services or a identical sign for similar goods or services (s10(2)).
   (iii) Identical or similar sign for dissimilar goods or service for which the registered mark has a *reputation* (s10(3)).
4. Infringement requires that the defendant use a sign in the course of trade. However, it is not necessary for the defendant to use the sign as a trade mark. If there is a use of the sign for business purposes and so as to indicate the origin of the goods or services, this will be deemed as a use of a sign in the course of trade (*Reed Executive v Reed Business Information* (2003) at para 51).
5. However, the use of sign in a course of trade may have nothing to do with identifying the origin of the goods or service to which it applies, but only for descriptive purposes. Under such a circumstance, the use of a sign in the trade for a descriptive purpose may not constitute a trade mark infringement.
6. For example, cards that showed the shirts of England football team players, whose shirts were carrying a registered logo of the Football Association, was not a use of the logo in relation to the shirts. Use of the registered mark as a business name for the different goods or services will not be an infringement *per se*.

# 8.3 THE THREE TYPES OF INFRINGEMENT

## 8.3.1 An identical sign for identical goods or services (s10(1) TMA 1994)

1. S10(1) TMA 1994 provides that it is a trade mark infringement to use a sign identical to the registered mark on identical goods or services within the specifications of the registered mark. A claimant is not liable to prove any likelihood of confusion.
2. The two marks will be identical if they are the same both in spelling and sound.
3. To decide whether two goods or services are identical, the court will refer to the key contents of the specification for the registered trade mark.

## 8.3.2 A similar sign for identical or similar goods or services or a identical sign for similar goods or services (s10(2) TMA 1994).

1. S10(2) TMA 1994 provides that where the two goods or services are similar, and/or two marks are similar, the claimant will have to prove that there is a likelihood of confusion on the part of the public.
2. Both the goods or services in question and the marks in question have to be assessed for the purpose of similarity. The question of whether goods or services are similar shall be settled before turning to the question whether the two signs are similar.
3. In practice, a registered mark with a reputation will attract more protection as a wider range of similar goods or services will be held by the courts to apply to the registered mark.
4. The following factors shall be considered when deciding whether there will be a likelihood of confusion by the public:

- the amount of use;
- the physical nature of the goods or services concerned;
- how they are sold; and
- how consumers might consider the competitiveness of goods or services.

5. The likelihood of association of the sign of the defendant with the registered trade mark by the public will constitute one kind of the likelihood of confusion by the public under s10(2) TMA 1994. The 'association' is a sub-set of 'confusion'.
6. In deciding whether there is a likelihood of association, the court will consider the following factors:
   - The feature of the markets for the goods and services in question.
   - Confusions arising in both written and oral usage.
   - Consumers' knowledge of the origin of the goods and services.
   - Nature of the Consumers affected.
7. A mere association of a sign with a non-similar registered trade mark by a 'fairly stupid or fairly uncaring' customer could be sufficient for finding a trade mark infringement by a UK court (*BP Amoco v Kelly* (2002)).
8. The considerations on a comparison of marks at the application stage are equally applicable to the trade mark infringement. The claimant has to show that the defendant used the sign to indicate the origin of its own goods or services in question.
9. The confusion must be judged from the perspective of the average consumer of the type of goods or services in question.
10. A 'global appreciation' test is now used. The average consumer is assumed to perceive a mark as a whole and not analyse it in detail. The more distinctive the earlier mark, the greater the likelihood of confusion.
11. Whether a mark has a strong distinctive character will not only be decided on the basis of generalised percentage of

recognition of the registered mark by the public. The courts will take into account the surrounding circumstances, such as how the two marks are represented to the general public, where they are displayed and what are the functions of the goods or services in question.

12. In summary, the court will look at the circumstances overall in order to determine whether there was a genuine and substantial likelihood of confusion by the relevant public. An 'association' cannot arise in most cases of comparative advertising, as once the comparison is made plain, there is no room for confusion.

### 8.3.3 Identical or similar sign for dissimilar goods or services for which the registered mark has a reputation (s10(3) TMA 1994)

1. S10(3) TMA 1994 provides that there will be an infringement by the defendant to use the same or a similar mark for dissimilar goods or services when:
   (a) the claimant has a registered trade mark with a 'reputation'; and
   (b) the use of the sign by the defendant is without due cause, which takes unfair advantage of or is detrimental to the distinctive character or repute of the registered mark.
2. This prevents a registered trade mark from being diluted through the use of the sign on the dissimilar goods or services by the person other than the proprietor of the registered trade mark. Such a type of infringement is supplemental to the national unfair competition regime.
3. However, the prevention of a dilution of a registered trade mark shall only be applied where there is sufficient cause for interfering with the freedom of all traders to compete their goods or services as best as they can.
4. There does not need to be any likelihood of confusion.
5. The detriment required for this type of infringement can be proved through 'blurring' or 'tarnishing'.

6. Especially under the English law, the courts have used the passing off action rather than the trade mark infringement action against occasional cases of 'dilution'.
7. To establish infringement, the registered mark has to have a 'reputation'. However, it does not have to be 'well-known' or 'famous'. The 'reputation' need only exist in part of the geographical area for which the registration pertains.
8. It is enough for a claimant to show that the use of sign by the defendant is taking unfair advantage of the registered trade mark, without showing that the registered mark owner is suffering detriment.
9. The conditions such as the lack of due cause, unfair advantage or detriment shall not be assumed to be present whenever there is dilution onto other goods. However, causing confusion to the origin of the goods or services in question by the defendant could, to the most extent, satisfy the above conditions.
10. In some cases, the unacceptable actions of misappropriation of goodwill could also satisfy the above conditions.
11. However, there should be a fine line between the misappropriation of goodwill and the acquisition of a monopoly on the registered trade mark by the proprietor for all trading uses. A *de minimus* advantage taken by a defendant shall not be sufficient for finding infringement (*Pebble Beach Co v Lombard Brands* (2003) at para 19).

## 8.4 USE OF A REGISTERED MARK TO IDENTIFY THE PROPRIETOR OR A LICENSEE OTHER THAN IN ACCORDANCE WITH HONEST PRACTICE

1. It was held by the courts that comparative advertising might help show objectively the merits of the various goods or services to customers – *Barclays Bank v RBS Advanta* (1996).

As a result, it shall only be prohibited where there are misleading statements in relation to the quality or other information of the goods or services in question.

2. S10(6) TMA 1994 provides that there is an exception to s10(1) infringement where the use of a registered mark is for the purpose of identifying goods or services as those of the registered trade mark owner or a licensee, provided that:
   (i) the reference to the registered trade mark owner is otherwise than in accordance with honest practise in industrial and commercial matter;
   (ii) is without due cause; and
   (iii) takes unfair advantage of, or is detrimental to, the distinctive character or repute of the mark.
3. A mere showing of an unfair advantage of the registered mark by a defendant in comparison advertising will not be enough to claim for this kind of infringement. A material dishonesty beyond a pure puffery by a defendant must be proven. In addition, a misleading usage of the registered mark as that required for the tort of injurious falsehood shall be proved as well.
4. The burden of proof lies with the claimant whose registered mark has been taken for comparison.
5. An objective test is taken in deciding whether there is a dishonest practise by reference to the reasonable reader of the advertisement, which may include different sectors of the public, provided they are substantial to the advertisement.
6. The general public is taken to know the ways of advertisers and to expect hyperbole. They will judge the advertisement as a whole. As a result, dishonesty will only be found when there is a significant misleading by the advertisement.

## 8.5 Limitations of Infringement Claims

1. The proceedings for infringement can only be made out when the registered trade mark has actually been granted to the proprietor.

2. S10(5) TMA 1994 provides that a person who actually applies a registered mark to material for labelling, packaging, business paper or advertising will contribute to the infringement if he knew or had reason to believe that the application of the registered mark was not authorised.

## 8.6 DEFENCES TO INFRINGEMENT

1. A defendant may defend a trade mark infringement claim through the following defences.

### 8.6.1 Conflicts between marks

1. S11(1) TMA 1994 provides that so long as a mark remains registered, use of it in its registered form cannot amount to infringement of any other mark.

### 8.6.2 Invalidity

1. The later mark owner may proceed for a declaration of invalidity on the relative or absolute ground of a prior registered mark pursuant to s47 TMA 1994. The relative or absolute ground shall be judged at the time of its registration.
2. Once the registered mark was declared invalid, the registration will be invalid from the outset in accordance with s47(5), (6) TMA 1994.
3. The defendant's ability to invalidate a prior registered mark by showing a prior right at the time of the application is subject to two limitations:
   (i) an owner of a senior mark or other rights cannot object to a registration after consenting to it; and
   (ii) the right to object may be lost if there is a statutory acquiescence, which will arise when a person with the prior right has been aware that the later registered mark has been used in the UK for a continuous period of five years.

4. Pursuant to the above two exceptions, a registered proprietor could not object to the usage of a registered mark by the senior owner (e.g. a defendant), while the senior owner may seek to revoke the registered trade mark for non-use or deceptive use.

## 8.7 Revocation

1. S46 TMA 1994 provides that a UK trade mark registration can be revoked on the ground that:
   (i) the registered mark is non-use; or
   (ii) the mark has become descriptive; or
   (iii) the mark has become deceptive.
2. S100 TMA 1994 imposes the burden of proof on the mark owner to provide the evidence of usage of the registered trade mark when there is a claim of revocation on the ground of non-use.
3. It is not necessary for an objector to prove any interest in the registered mark.
4. If the objection is made out only for some of the goods or services within the specifications there will be revocation for them alone. In deciding what is the fair specification of goods or services in considering the use made, the courts must take a 'reasonably informed customer' test.
5. To affix the registered mark to goods or packaging purely for export from the UK will be a sufficient use. A small number of sales may also be sufficient for a genuine use. A distinction must be made between a genuine effort to start trading and purely colourable use designed to maintain the rights alive.
6. There will be no revocation if any of the following exceptions applies:
   (i) there is a use of mark that differs from the registered mark only in some elements which do not alter the distinctive character of the registered mark.
   (ii) There has been a resumption of use before the application to revoke is made.

(iii) There are proper reasons for non-use, i.e. any reason that is apt, acceptable, reasonable and justifiable in all of the circumstances.

7. A revocation could be made out if the mark has become the common name in the trade for the goods or services in question. It will be extremely dangerous for a mark to be given a generic description in a dictionary.
8. The courts use the 'relevant trade' test to decide whether the registered trade mark has become a generic description of the goods or services to which it applies. The test refers to what the relevant trade understands for the registered mark, but not the general public.
9. Where the use of the registered trade mark has mislead the public, particularly for the nature, quality or geographical origin of the goods or services in question, the registration of the mark can be revoked.
10. Misleading could occur when the registered mark was used for the first time as well as when there was a change in use or assignment or licensing (*Scandecor Development v Scandecor Marketing* (2002)).
11. The test for deceptive ground is whether the public could be misled by the blameworthy conduct of the registered proprietor. No malice will need to be proved in such a case.

## 8.8 LIMITATION USES OF THE MARK BY AN UNAUTHORISED USER

1. S11(1), (2) TMA 1994 provides that the use of a mark in accordance with the following honest practices in industrial and commercial matters will not constitute an infringement:
   (i) a person's own name or address;
   (ii) indications of kind, time of production or rendering, or other characteristics of goods or services;
   (iii) the mark itself as the accessories or spare parts of goods or services, indicating the purposes of goods or services.

2. The defendant's solely descriptive use of the registered mark could be excused as such a use may be expected by the general public. As a result, a use of the registered mark not of trade mark nature is more likely to be excused under s11 TMA 1994.
3. The test for the 'honest practice' is an objective test. The courts will look at the likely effect of the use of the registered mark by the defendant to decide whether he has acted honestly.
4. In addition, s11(3) TMA 1994 provides that there will not be an infringement if there is a purely local use of an unregistered trade mark or other sign which is itself protectable as an 'earlier right'.

## 8.9 Exhaustion of Right

1. S12 TMA 1994 provides that the trade mark rights of a registered proprietor will be exhausted once the goods or services are on the market.
2. The exhaustion rule is applied to the national territory as well as the Community territory.
3. However, the exhaustion rule is subject to the exception where there exist legitimate reasons for the proprietor to oppose further commercialisation of goods or services, particularly where the goods or services have been changed or impaired after they are put on the market.

# CHAPTER 9

# PASSING OFF

Passing off is primarily from case law and not from statute. It is extremely flexible and wide ranging.

A typical set of guidelines for passing off is this from *Warnink v Townend* (1979)

(a) a misrepresentation
(b) made by a trader in the course of trade
(c) to prospective customers of his or ultimate consumers of goods supplied by him
(d) which is calculated to injure the business or goodwill of another trader (if foreseeable)
(e) which causes actual damage to a business or goodwill of a trader.

*Reckitt and Colman Products* (1990), demonstrating these guidelines, required only three factors – the claimant's goodwill, a misrepresentation as to the goods, and likely damage

Misrepresentation may be:

- written or oral
- caused by suggestive conduct
- in relation to source

## 9.1 WHAT IS PASSING OFF?

1. Passing off protects the goodwill of a product. In *Reddaway v Banham* (1986) Lord Halsbury said:
   'Nobody has any right to represent his goods as the goods of somebody else'.
2. The requirement of goodwill indicates something more than merely copying the name or style of a trader. Reputation may occur through constant use, as in *Reddaway* where the phrase 'Camel Hair Belting' was used by the claimant for 12 years. Thus, if a trader has just entered into business, that trader may not have sufficient goodwill.

3. Goodwill should exist at the time when the defendant's acts that are complained of begin.

## 9.2 The Assessment of Passing Off

1. Adapting *Spalding and Bros v AW Gamage* (1915), Lord Diplock in *Warnink v Townend* (1979) (the 'Advocaat' case) set out a five stage test, which determined that there must be:

> **(a) a misrepresentation;**
> **(b) made by a trader in the course of trade;**
> **(c) to prospective customers of his or ultimate consumers of goods supplied by him;**
> **(d) which is calculated to injure the business or goodwill of another trader (if foreseeable);**
> **(e) which causes actual damage to a business or goodwill of a trader.**

2. However, note that these were guidelines, and as such, are not set in stone. Lord Fraser in the same case set out slightly different ones:

> **(a) The claimant's business consists of selling in England a class of goods to which the name in question applies.**
> **(b) The class of goods is clearly defined, and is distinguished in the minds of the public from other similar goods.**
> **(c) Because of the reputation of the product, goodwill is attached to the name.**
> **(d) The goodwill is of substantial value.**
> **(e) The claimant has suffered, or will suffer, substantial damage to his property.**

3. Lord Oliver reduced the guidelines to three items in *Reckitt and Colman Products* (1990), requiring the claimant's goodwill, a misrepresentation as to the goods, and likely damage. Note the fluidity of the test.

## 9.3 MISREPRESENTATION

1. Misrepresentation is not simply a question of whether there is confusion, but whether the use of the defendant's name, in conjunction with the goods, make out to the consumer that the goods were the claimants, or that it could harm the claimant's goodwill.

### 9.3.1 Written or oral statements

1. Misrepresentation may arise by written or oral statements, or because of the similarity of the goods in question.
2. In *Associated Press v Insert Media* (1991) it was held that inserting advertisements inside a newspaper after delivery to a newsagents made them appear as if they were the claimant's.
3. In *British Telecommunications v One In A Million* (1998), the same was held in relation to registering domain names where the goodwill was held by another.

### 9.3.2 Suggestive conduct

1. Misrepresentation may be indicated by certain suggestive conduct.
2. There could be misrepresentation as to quality.
3. In *Spalding*, the claimant sold and manufactured footballs, and the defendant had obtained some old stock. The defendant sold them as if they were new, improved footballs. An action for passing off was upheld. Note that this could permit the use of passing off to control parallel imports.

### 9.3.3 Misrepresentation as to source

1. Misrepresentation as to source is the traditional form of misrepresentation.
2. The 'get up' of a product, namely its packaging, may be protected by passing off.

3. In *Reckitt and Colman,* the Gif Lemon was held to be protected by passing off, where the defendant sold lemon juice in a similar, larger container with a flat side and green cap. Lord Oliver held there was a misrepresentation.

### 9.3.4 Misrepresentation which deceives

1. The misrepresentation should deceive the general public at large – *Marengo v Daily Sketch* (1948).
2. However, if the goods are available only to a *portion* of the general public, then the view of that portion will be taken into account instead.
3. The nature of the customers in question will depend on the facts of the case – note the consumer orientated approach in *Reckitt and Coleman,* where Lord Oliver said the 'customers have to be taken as they are found'.
4. The test for the quantity of the public required to be confused has been stated as requiring that 'enough [of the public] are [fooled] for enough of the time'. This may be assumed to refer to a substantial part of the public (*Lego v Lemelstrich* (1983)). Note that the public does not have to be knowledgeable about the product concerned (*Bollinger v Costa Bravo Wine (No 2)* (1961)). As *Reckitt* noted, consumers will take less notice of some products than others.
5. Acquiescence may negate misrepresentation (*Vine Products* (1969)).

## 9.4 MADE BY A TRADER IN THE COURSE OF TRADE

1. Originally, the width of passing off was narrow. It used to be the case that the claimant and defendant had to be in the same business – *Clark v Freeman.* This is no longer so. 'In the course of trade' does not mean the same type of trade.

2. Trade no longer even has to be associated with commercial activity. In *British Diabetic Association v Diabetic Society* (1996), it was held that a charity could fit within the definition.
3. Note there is a longstanding issue with names. Use of names may not fall within the 'course of trade' – *McCullough v Lewis* (1948).

## 9.5 Geographical Area

1. The geographical area covered by goodwill may vary from case to case. In *Associated Newspapers* (2003), it was noted that the reputation of the newspaper concerned was more pronounced in the South East.
2. Some cases have suggested that customers in the UK are not necessary to show goodwill, such as *Alain Beradin v Pavilion* (1967). Others have – *Panhard v Panhard* (1901).

## 9.6 Actual Damage

1. Actual damage, as under the *Spalding* test, must be shown. This can be difficult to achieve and many cases fail under this heading.
2. Some cases such as *Irvine v Talksport* (2003) have downplayed the importance of the requirement, though that is not to say it is not important. In *Irvine*, the issue was that of *potential* damages, namely lost profit. However, failure to provide *any* evidence of damage is likely to be fatal to the case of a claimant – *Arsenal Football Club v Reed* (2001).

## 9.7 Reverse Passing Off

1. This is where a trader seeks to claim the benefit from another trader's goods or services. This should be done to enhance that defendant trader's business.
2. The extent of the doctrine is uncertain. It is unlikely to apply to a company simply reselling products. It may apply,

at least, in relation to where a defendant company presents someone else's goods as their own. In *Bristol Conservatories* (1989), the defendant showed potential customers leaflets which led them to believe they were their own, when instead they were the claimant's.

3. Association may lead to reverse passing off. In *John Robert Powers School v Denyse Bernadette Tessensohn* (1995) leaving study notes on a shelf easily accessible gave the impression that the notes were the defendant's.

## 9.8 FLEXIBILITY OF THE DOCTRINE

1. The most important aspect of passing off is its flexibility. It may be said to incorporate many more aspects than, say, registered trade marks.
2. An example of the flexibility of the doctrine is shown by *Irvine v Talksport* (2003). Here the doctrine was applied to the issue of endorsement. A Formula 1 driver was shown listening to Talksport on a radio, but this was a doctored photo. The driver sued and succeeded.

# CHAPTER 10

# BREACH OF CONFIDENCE

**The test for confidence is typically that:**
**(i) there must be information that has the necessary quality to be confidential**
**(ii) the information must have been disclosed in circumstances implying an obligation of confidence.**
**(iii) there must be unauthorised use of that information.**

**A typical test for assessing confidence is:**
**(i) the owner must be under the belief that disclosure of the information is prejudicial to his interests and advantageous to his rivals;**
**(ii) the owner must believe that the information is secret and confidential;**
**(iii) these two beliefs must be reasonable; and**
**(iv) the information must be judged in the light of prevailing trade or industry usage and practices.**

**The usual intellectual property remedies are available for breach of confidence actions. These include injunction, account of profits, and order for delivery up.**

## 10.1 INTRODUCTION

1. The law of confidence helps to protect secrets and confidential information.
2. It has its origin in common law and equity.
3. The Human Rights Act 1998 now offers statutory recognition to the right of privacy. However, the law of breach of confidence in the context of intellectual property is meant to protect secrets and confidential information.
4. The law of confidence often acts complementary to copyright law and patent law. For example, if someone narrates the idea for a TV programme to the producer, the latter would be under an obligation not to exploit the idea

without the permission of the person who narrated it, subject to certain conditions (*Fraser v Thames Television Ltd* (1984)). Copyright law will not afford this protection, as ideas are not protected unless expressed in some tangible form.

5. Similarly, the law of breach of confidence also helps inventors or patent applicants by imposing a duty of confidence on those whom the applicant had to describe the relevant invention prior to a formal patent application. Accordingly, the Patents Act 1977 expressly states that publication made in breach of confidence will not invalidate a patent application.
6. The law of breach of confidence has been applied in personal relationships as well, such as husband and wife (*Argyll v Argyll* (1967)), between friends (*Stevens v Avery* (1988)) and also to state secrets (*Attorney-General v The Observer Ltd* (1989)).

## 10.2 Conditions for Confidence

1. There are three main conditions to be satisfied for imposing a duty of confidence (*Coco v AN Clark (Engineers) Ltd* (1969)):

**(i) There must be information that has necessary quality to be confidential.**

↓

**(ii) The information must have been disclosed in circumstances implying an obligation of confidence.**

↓

**(iii) There must be unauthorised use of that information.**

2. Each of these three conditions will be analysed in further detail below.

### 10.2.1 Confidential information

1. 'Information' can include almost everything, irrespective of whether it is industrial, personal, political, literary or artistic.
2. However, trivial information will not be protected (*Faccenda Chicken v Fowler* (1986)) although this does not mean personal secrets or gossips are never covered by the law (*Barrymore v News Group Newspapers Ltd* (1997)).
3. Information must have the necessary quality of confidence about it to be protected, i.e. it must not be common knowledge or in the public domain (*Saltman Engineering Co Ltd v Campbell Engineering Co Ltd* (1948)).
4. A four-prong test was suggested in *Thomas Marshal Exports Ltd v Guinle* (1979) in order to determine if the information has the necessary quality of confidence:
   (i) the owner must be under the belief that disclosure of the information is prejudicial to his interests and advantageous to his rivals;
   (ii) the owner must believe that the information is secret and confidential;
   (iii) these two beliefs must be reasonable; and
   (iv) the information must be judged in the light of prevailing trade or industry usage and practices.
5. Once the information becomes available in the public domain, it ceases to be confidential except under the 'springboard doctrine'.

### 10.2.2 Springboard doctrine

1. Once information becomes public knowledge it is no longer capable of being treated as confidential.
2. This general rule is subject to the exception of what is known as the springboard doctrine.
3. The purpose of this provision is to ensure that a person who has obtained information in confidence is not allowed to use it as a springboard for activities detrimental to the person who made the confidential communication. The person who

obtained the information will still be bound by a duty of confidence, even when all the features have been published and are available to the public (*Terrapin Ltd v Builders' Supply Co (Hayes) Ltd* (1960)).

4. However, it will be unfair to hold the springboard doctrine against the defendant eternally, therefore it will only be granted for a reasonable period of time.

## 10.3 Obligation of Confidence

1. The second condition of *Coco v Clark* is that information must have been imparted in circumstances implying a duty of confidence.
2. There are numerous circumstances that can imply an obligation of confidence.
3. This is not limited to a contract or such other formalities, and in fact has been extended to relationships based on trust, friendship and marriage as well as pre-contractual disclosures.
4. Where there is a contract between the parties, it is not usually difficult to imply an obligation of confidence. In fact often there will be express contractual clauses addressing this.
5. The advantage of using a contract is that it can clearly demarcate the boundaries of the obligation being imposed, although this will not preclude any equitable obligations being imposed additionally.
6. When there is no express creation of obligation such as in a contract, it can be implied from the relevant circumstances. This can include the relationship between the parties, circumstances in which the information was disclosed, etc.
7. Fiduciary relationships such as partnerships and trusts have also been held to be relevant in determining a duty of confidence (*Morison v Moat* (1851), *Cranleigh Precision Engineering v Bryant* (1964)).

8. A third party who is not a direct recipient of the information from the owner has an obligation of confidence if he has knowledge that the information was confidential (*Prince Albert v Strange* (1849), *Morison v Moat* (1851)).

### 10.3.1 Employment contracts

1. Employment contracts usually have express terms imposing an obligation of confidence.
2. In the absence of any express term, obligations of the employee in respect of the use and disclosure of information are subject to implied terms, which impose a duty of good faith of fidelity (*Faccenda Chicken v Fowler* (1986)). It was also observed in *Faccenda* that the extent of the duty of good faith will vary according to the nature of the contract.
3. The employee will usually be under the obligation to protect trade secrets, even if this is not an express term in the contract (*Hivac Ltd v Park Royal Scientific Instruments Ltd* (1946)).
4. There is no obligation on the employee with respect to unlawful or illegal activities of his employer.
5. The duty of confidence may run beyond the termination of employment as well in some circumstances. It may either be part of the employment contract, or an implied continuing duty of confidence.
6. The employee may also acquire information (confidential or otherwise) during the employment that may be used post-employment.
7. In order to determine which of these two categories the information will fall into, the test used is whether the information in question is fairly considered part of the employee's stock of knowledge which a person of ordinary honesty and intelligence would recognise to be the property of their former employer, in which case the information is regarded as confidential and will be protected. Otherwise, the information is treated as know-how and cannot be protected,

falling into the general knowledge or know-how of the employee's own trade.

8. Case law suggests that an employee can be restrained from competing with the employer using the 'skills and knowledge' acquired during the course of the employment relationship within reasonable limits of time and space after the termination of employment. But this should not be unreasonable and must be in accordance with competition law, i.e. the employee should be able to use his skills and knowledge for his own benefit as well (*Faccenda Chicken v Fowler* (1986)).

### 10.3.2 Unauthorised use of information

1. The third requirement of *Coco v Clark* is that there must be unauthorised use of confidential information for an action for breach of confidence.
2. 'Use' will include disclosure of information. It is not relevant if the subsequent use of the information by the recipient has resulted in creating a similar work as the owner; the stress is on 'use' rather than the outcome of the use.
3. In order to establish unauthorised use, it is a pre-requisite to show that the defendant's information came from the claimant.
4. Partial use of information may also amount to breach in certain circumstances.

## 10.4 DEFENCES

1. There are a few defences available to breach of confidence, although the most important one is the public interest defence.
2. The Human Rights Act 1998 has accorded a greater significance to the public interest defence, especially with the statutory recognition it offers to the right to privacy and freedom of expression.

3. It is permitted to publish the information if it is in the public interest (*Lion Laboratories Ltd v Evans & Others* (1984), *W v Edgell* (1990)).
4. The information must clearly be in the public interest. This is further subject to the requirement that the disclosure must be made to a proper recipient.
5. Thus, it will not always be a defence to disclose information to the press where other options are available (*Attorney-General v The Observer Ltd* (1989)).
6. The court will also balance the public interest with any other rights involved, including the right of confidence.

## 10.5 Remedies

1. The usual intellectual property remedies are available for breach of confidence actions as well.
2. These include injunction, account of profits, and order for delivery up.
3. The most usual remedy that the plaintiff seeks is injunction, but if the information is already in the public domain it will be impractical and an injunction will not be granted.
4. Damages can be awarded where the breach of confidence is also a breach of contract.
5. Damages will be awarded to put the claimant in the original position had there been no breach of confidence.
6. Account of profits is available where the obligation is non-contractual and is based purely on equity (*Spycatcher* (1990)).
7. Delivery up or destruction of material also is available as a remedy in an action for breach of confidence.

CHAPTER 11

# INTRODUCTION AND THE NATURE OF COPYRIGHT

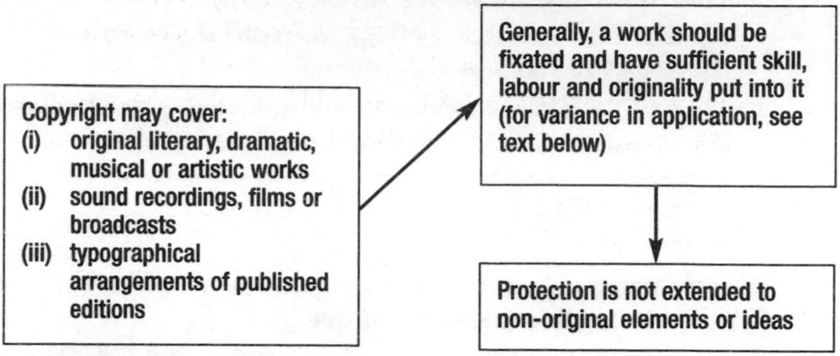

Copyright may cover:
(i) original literary, dramatic, musical or artistic works
(ii) sound recordings, films or broadcasts
(iii) typographical arrangements of published editions

Generally, a work should be fixated and have sufficient skill, labour and originality put into it (for variance in application, see text below)

Protection is not extended to non-original elements or ideas

The author of a literary, dramatic, musical or artistic work is the person who creates it. But if an employee in the course of his employment creates the work, the employer will be the first owner of copyright in the work

Note there is a *sui generis* database right (a database may not be protected by copyright law if its content is not original, but it could be protected by a *sui generis* right designed for that purpose)

## 11.1 INTRODUCTION

### 11.1.1 Copyright and the law

1. Copyright protects original work from being copied or reproduced without authorisation.
2. The governing law of copyright in the UK is the Copyright, Designs and Patents Act 1988 (CDPA 1988).
3. There is no copyright in ideas. Ideas must be expressed in some tangible form for copyright to subsist.

### 11.1.2 Registration of copyright

1. There is no requirement of registration for copyright. Copyright accrues from the moment a work is expressed in some tangible format; all that is needed to prove ownership is to produce original creation of the work with proof of authorship. The author should either be a qualifying person or the work must be first published in a Convention country.
2. To be a qualifying person, the author must be, at the material time, a British citizen, subject or protected person, a British Dependent Territories citizen, a British National (Overseas), a British Overseas citizen, or must have been resident or domiciled in a Convention country at the material time (s154 CDPA 1988).

### 11.1.3 Where does copyright subsist?

1. Copyright subsists in (s1 CDPA 1988):

**(i) original literary, dramatic, musical or artistic works;**
**(ii) sound recordings, films or broadcasts;**
**(iii) typographical arrangements of published editions.**

2. Copyright subsists only in original works.

### 11.1.4 What constitutes work?

1. There is no statutory definition of 'work', but case law establishes that the author must have expended a minimum amount of effort.

### 11.1.5 Trivial works

1. There is no copyright in trivial works.
2. A single word was refused copyright protection in *Exxon v Exxon Insurance* (1982).

3. Similarly, titles and names also do not usually qualify for copyright protection (*Francis Day and Hunter v Twentieth Century Fox* (1940)).

### 11.1.6 Duration of copyright

1. The duration of copyright depends according to the type of work.

## 11.2 HISTORY OF COPYRIGHT LAW

### 11.2.1 The 16th century

1. Copyright protection dates back to the 16th century.
2. Authors had the option of registering their books with the Stationer's Company, which granted them a right to prevent others from reproducing the work.
3. This right was only for books and ran until perpetuity.

### 11.2.2 The 18th century

1. The right was extended to engravings in 1734 through the Engraving Copyright Act.

### 11.2.3 The 19th century

1. There were around 15 different copyright related Acts in the statute books by the 19th century.
2. The UK signed the Berne Copyright Convention in 1885. This necessitated changes and consolidation of various Acts prior to 1885 in order to bring UK law in conformity to the international standards as envisaged by the Berne Convention.

### 11.2.4 The 20th and 21st century

1. This resulted in the creation of the 1911 Copyright Act, which repealed and replaced all previous copyright-related acts and also abolished the common law copyright that provided for indefinite protection for unpublished works.
2. The 1911 Act was further modified following the amendments to the Berne Convention in 1951, resulting in the Copyright Act 1956.
3. Technological advances called for further modifications to the 1956 Copyright Act, which was achieved through a number of amending statutes.
4. The Whitford Committee was appointed in 1973 to study the state of copyright law in light of technological changes, whose recommendations eventually led to the Copyright, Designs and Patents Act (CDPA) 1988.
5. Further amendments were made to the CDPA 1988 to comply with EC Directives for the protection of software, semiconductor chip topography rights as well as for the harmonisation of copyright duration.
6. The UK signed the Agreement on Trade Related Aspects of Intellectual Property Rights (TRIPS) in April 1994, which seeks to establish minimum standards of protection for intellectual property rights.
7. The effect of this was copyright protection to computer programs in object code or source code form, protection of database and rental rights.

## 11.3 FIXATION

### 11.3.1 Expressing in a material form

1. One of the basic principles of copyright law is that there is no copyright in ideas; ideas must be expressed in some material form for copyright to subsist (*University of London Press v University Tutorial Press* (1916)).

2. A literary, musical or dramatic work must be recorded in writing or otherwise (s3(2) CDPA 1988) for copyright to subsist.
3. Writing includes any form of notation or code, whether by hand or otherwise, and irrespective of the medium or the method by which it is recorded (s178 CDPA 1988).

### 11.3.2 When copyright comes into existence

1. Copyright comes into existence at the time at which it is recorded (*Walter v Lane* (1900)).
2. When a work is recorded, copyright may subsist both in the recording as well as in the underlying work (s3(3) CDPA 1988).

## 11.4 ORIGINALITY

1. For copyright to subsist in literary, dramatic, artistic or musical works, it must be original.
2. The author must have expended sufficient degree of skill, labour and judgment to establish originality.
3. The requirement of originality applies to literary, musical, dramatic and artistic works only, and not to sound recordings, films or broadcasts.
4. In *University of London Press v University Tutorial Press* (1916), Petersen J noted that the word 'original' does not mean that the work must be the expression of original or inventive thought. The important aspect is that the work must not be copied from another work – it should originate from the author.
5. Thus, there will be copyright protection for a work even if it has been derived from other sources, provided that the author has expended sufficient skill, labour and judgement into it.
6. In *University of London Press v University Tutorial Press* (1916), it was held that examination papers involved 'selection, judgement and experience'.

7. In *Ladbroke (Football) v William Hill* (1964), the House of Lords held that coupons for football pools constituted original literary works.

## 11.5 LITERARY WORKS

### 11.5.1 Definition of literary work

1. A literary work includes any work other than a dramatic or musical work, which is spoken, sung or written (s3(1) CDPA 1988).
2. While there is no requirement that the work should actually have literary value (*University of London Press Ltd v University Tutorial Press Ltd* (1916)), it must be more than *de minimis.*
3. Single words will not attract copyright protection (*Exxon Corpn v Exxon Insurance Consultants International Ltd* (1982)).
4. Literary works include tables and compilations other than databases; computer programs; preparatory design material for computer programs; and databases.

### 11.5.2 Databases

1. The Database Directive harmonised the copyright for databases as literary works.
2. A database comprises a collection of independent works, data or other materials, which are arranged in a systematic or methodical way and are individually accessible by electronic or other means (s3A CDPA 1988).
3. In order to meet the requirement of originality, the database must, whether by reason of the selection itself, or arrangement of the contents, constitute the author's own intellectual creation (s3A CDPA 1988).

# 11.6 Dramatic Works

## 11.6.1 Definition of dramatic work

1. S3(1) CDPA 1988 defines dramatic works as works of dance or mime.
2. Dramatic works will also usually include plays written for the theatre, cinema or television screenplays.

## 11.6.2 Distinction between a dramatic work and literary work

1. The essential distinction between a dramatic work and literary work is that a dramatic work is something that is capable of being performed by acting or dancing (*Green v Broadcasting Corporation of New Zealand* (1989)), whereas a literary work is something that can be merely read out or recited.
2. It is important to note that copyright in a dramatic work will only cover the work as such, the way it is written or printed and does not extend to the manner in which it is performed or is interpreted by the person performing it (*Tate v Fullbrook* (1908)).

# 11.7 Musical Works

## 11.7.1 Definition of musical works

1. Musical works consist of music, exclusive of any words or action intended to be sung, spoken or performed with the music.
2. The words or action that is excluded from the definition of musical works may qualify as literary or dramatic works, which qualifies for separate copyright.
3. Thus, a song can have more than one copyright, one for the lyric and a different copyright for musical notes.

### 11.7.2 Quality of musical works

1. The actual quality or merit of music is not relevant, as long as the sounds are not too simple and trivial so as not to constitute a work at all to obtain copyright protection.
2. Copyright extends to secondary musical works as well.

## 11.8 Artistic Works

### 11.8.1 Definition of artistic works

1. Artistic works mean a graphic work, photograph, sculpture or collage irrespective or artistic quality, a work of architecture being a building or a model for a building or a work of artistic craftsmanship.
2. Artistic works are protected irrespective of actual artistic merit, except in the case of works of artistic craftsmanship, where the courts may be required to make an artistic judgment (*Vermaat and Powell v Boncrest Ltd* (2001)).

### 11.8.2 Graphic works

1. 'Graphic work' will include any painting, drawing, diagram, map, chart or plan and any engraving, etching, lithograph, wood cut or similar work.

### 11.8.3 Photographic works

1. 'Photograph' is defined as a recording of light or other radiation on any medium on which an image is produced or from which an image may by any means be produced, and is not part of a film.

### 11.8.4 Buildings which attract protection as artistic works

1. Buildings also attract protection as artistic works. This is essentially an indirect copyright protection which originates from any copyright in the plans for them (*Pearce v Ove Arup Partnership Ltd* (1999)).

### 11.8.5 Originality

1. Artistic works must be original to qualify for copyright protection.
2. Originality is determined through the 'skill and labour' test, as is the case with literary works.
3. 'Artistic craftsmanship' is not defined in CDPA 1988, and has been subject to difficulties with regard to the interpretation of the definition by courts (*George Hensher v Restawile* (1976)).

## 11.9 Sound Recordings and Films

### 11.9.1 Sound recording

1. A sound recording is defined in s5(1) CDPA 1988 as: 'a recording of sounds from which the sounds may be reproduced; or a recording of the whole or any part of a literary, dramatic or musical work, from which sounds reproducing the work or part may be produced regardless of the medium on which or the method by which the recording is made and the sound is reproduced.'

### 11.9.2 Film

1. A film is defined as a recording on any medium from which a moving image may by any means be produced.
2. This definition of films covers video, television and movies.

3. There is no requirement of originality for sound recordings or films, but copyright will not subsist in a copy taken from a previous sound recording or film (s5(2) CDPA 1988).

## 11.10 Broadcasts

### 11.10.1 Definition of a broadcast

1. A broadcast is a transmission by wireless telegraphy of visual images, sounds or other information that is transmitted for presentation to members of the public or that the public can lawfully receive (s6(1)(a), (b) CDPA 1988).
2. Reception of a broadcast also includes reception of a broadcast relayed by means of a telecommunications system (s6(5) CDPA 1988).

### 11.10.2 Encrypted transmission

1. An encrypted transmission will be regarded as capable of being lawfully received by members of the public only if authorised decoding equipment has been provided.

## 11.11 Published Editions

### 11.11.1 Typographical arrangement

1. Copyright subsists in the typographical arrangement of a published edition.
2. What is published must be the whole or part of a literary, dramatic or musical work.

### 11.11.2 What part of a typographical arrangement is protected?

1. It is only the typographical arrangement that is protected. What is being published may have a separate copyright in itself.

2. A typographical arrangement that merely reproduces a previously published edition will not acquire a fresh copyright.

## 11.12 RELATED RIGHTS

### 11.12.1 *Sui generis* – rights for databases

1. Some databases may not meet the standard of originality to be afforded copyright protection.
2. In this case the database can be protected by virtue of the *sui generis* database right.
3. The Database Directive which was incorporated into UK law by Part III of the Copyright and Rights in Databases Regulations 1997 grants a property right in a database whether or not it qualifies for a copyright work.
4. The definition of database will include:
   'a collection of independent works, data or other materials arranged in a systematic or methodical way and individually accessible by electronic or other means'.
5. A database can also be recognised as literary work, and thus afforded copyright protection.
6. For this the database must be original and the contents and the arrangement of the database must be a result of the author's own intellectual creation.
7. In any case, all databases are protected by the new database right irrespective of whether they qualify for copyright protection or not.
8. To qualify for database rights the data must have been assembled through substantial investment in obtaining, verifying and presenting the contents (*British Horseracing Board Ltd v William Hill Organisation* (2001)).
9. The duration of database rights is for 15 years from 1st January of the year following the date of completion of its making, or the first making public of the database within the 15-year period from its making.

10. Where the author of a database is not an individual, the author is defined as the maker of the database.
11. The maker is the person who has invested in obtaining, verifying or presenting the contents.
12. Makers must be either nationals of EEA, or in cases of companies and organisations incorporated within the EEA in order to qualify for the database right protection.

### 11.12.2 Performer's rights

1. Copyright works are often performed by actors and musicians.
2. Such performances have been subject to bootlegging, which called for increased protection for performers and the original recordings.
3. Bootleg recordings are recordings of live performances made without consent.
4. This seriously undermines the economic interests of the performer as well as the authorised recorders.
5. Therefore, performers have been granted a new transferable property right in relation to performances, which is a related right in addition to copyright.
6. Performance right also includes the right to prevent unauthorised recordings of the performance.
7. Performance means one of the following categories of live performance (s180(2) CDPA 1988):
   (a) dramatic performance;
   (b) a musical performance;
   (c) a reading or recitation of literary work;
   (d) a performance of a variety act or similar presentation.
8. A performance qualifies for protection if it is given by a qualifying individual or if takes place in a qualifying country (s181 CDPA 1988).
9. The rights in performance last for 50 years from the end of the calendar year in which the performance takes place, or if a recording is released within that period, for 50 years from

the end of the calendar year in which it is released (s191 CDPA 1988).

## 11.13 Duration of Copyright

### 11.13.1 Literary, dramatic, musical and artistic works (s12 CDPA 1988)

1. These are protected for the author's life plus 70 years from the end of the calendar year in which the author dies.
2. There are certain exceptions to this general rule of life plus 70 years.
3. For works of unknown authorships copyright expires 70 years after the work is made available to the public.
4. Computer generated works qualify for a 70-year period for copyright protection from the time the work was made.
5. Duration of crown copyright is 125 years or 70 years from commercial publication, whichever is the shorter period (s163(3) CDPA 1988).

### 11.13.2 Sound recordings and films (s13 CDPA 1988)

1. Copyrights in sound recording and films last for 70 years from the end of the calendar year of making for unreleased versions, and for 70 years from the end of calendar year of release for released versions.
2. 'Release' is analogous to the concept of being 'made available to the public' as is the case for literary works.

### 11.13.3 Broadcasts and cable programmes (s14 CDPA 1988)

1. Copyright in broadcasts and cable programmes last until 70 years from the end of the calendar year when the broadcast was first made or the cable programme was first included in a cable programme service.

### 11.13.4 Published editions (s15 CDPA 1988)

1. Copyright in the typographical arrangement of published editions lasts until 25 years from the end of the year in which the edition is first published.

## 11.14 OWNERSHIP OF COPYRIGHT

### 11.14.1 Literary, dramatic, musical and artistic works

1. The author of a literary, dramatic, musical or artistic work is the person who creates it (s9(1) CDPA 1988).
2. This statutory exception applies to films since the 1996 Copyright Regulations came into force.
3. But if an employee in the course of his employment creates the work, the employer will be the first owner of copyright in the work (s11(2) CDPA 1988).
4. Whether the work was carried out in the course of employment depends on the status of the employee.
5. An 'employee' is defined in s178(1) CDPA 1988 as someone employed under a contract of service or of apprenticeship.
6. If the author was under a contract of service when the work was created the copyright will stay with the employer (*Beloff v Pressdram* (1973)).
7. If the author was commissioned to create the work under a contract for service the copyright will stay with the author.
8. Copyright for commissioned works stays with the author, subject to an express or implied term to the contrary (*Robin Ray v Classic FM plc* (1998)).

### 11.14.2 Course of employment

1. In the case of an employee creating a work in the course of employment, the employer is the owner of the work. This

applies to copyright in a literary, dramatic, musical or artistic work or a film.

2. There are three conditions to this provision: the author must be employed; the work was created during the course of the employment; and there are no agreements between the parties contrary to this.
3. 'Course of the employment' means duties and work which are carried out as part of the job description or contract.
4. However, it is difficult to lay down a rigid standard for this, as duties of employment can vary according to change in circumstances (*Stephenson Jordan and Harrison v MacDonald Evans* (1952)).

### 11.14.3 Other works

1. The copyright for sound recordings and films stays with the person by whom the arrangements necessary for the making of the recording or film are undertaken.
2. The author of a broadcast is the person who makes it (s9(2)(b) CDPA 1988).

# CHAPTER 12

# INFRINGEMENT AND DEFENCES

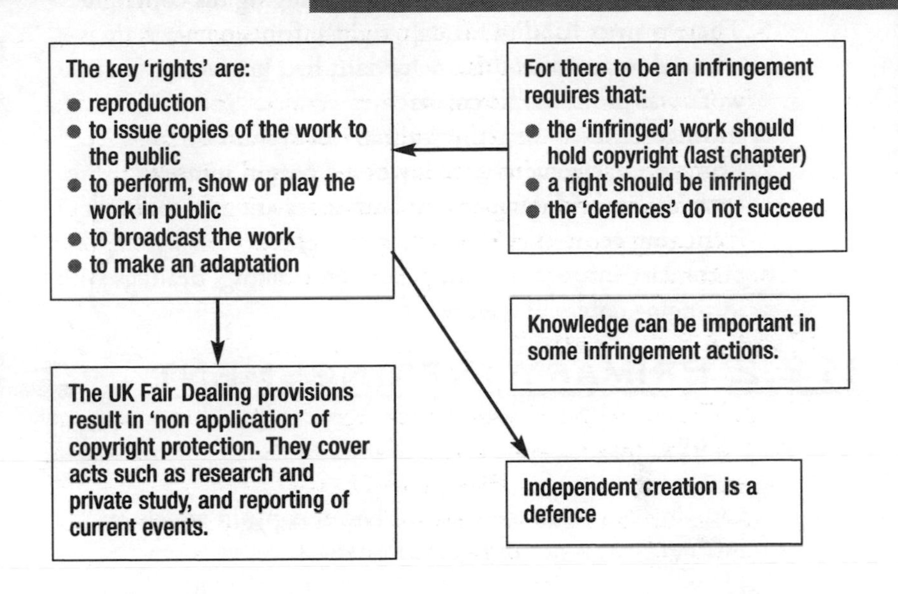

The key 'rights' are:
● reproduction
● to issue copies of the work to the public
● to perform, show or play the work in public
● to broadcast the work
● to make an adaptation
For there to be an infringement requires that:
● the 'infringed' work should hold copyright (last chapter)
● a right should be infringed
● the 'defences' do not succeed
Knowledge can be important in some infringement actions.
The UK Fair Dealing provisions result in 'non application' of copyright protection. They cover acts such as research and private study, and reporting of current events.
Independent creation is a defence


## 12.1 INTRODUCTION

**1.** The CDPA 1998 grants certain exclusive rights to copyright owners to do, or authorise others to do, acts in the UK in relation to those works (s16):

> **(I)** to copy the work;
> **(ii)** to issue copies of the work to the public;
> **(iii)** to perform, show or play the work in public;
> **(iv)** to broadcast the work or include it in a cable programme service;
> **(v)** to make an adaptation of the work or do any of the above in relation to an adaptation.

**2.** These rights extend to any adaptation of the work also.

3. An adaptation will be protected as an original copyright work in itself.
4. The CDPA 1998 effectively gives the owner of copyright a negative right to stop others from infringing his copyright.
5. There is strict liability for copyright infringement; there is no need to prove that the defendant had knowledge that the work was protected by copyright.
6. Infringement can be either primary or secondary.
7. Primary infringement occurs when a person himself commits an infringing act, or authorises another to do an infringing act restricted by the copyright.
8. Secondary infringement is, generally speaking, dealings with infringing copies of a work.

## 12.2 Primary Infringement

### 12.2.1 Copying

1. Copying can be an identical verbatim copy, in which case infringement is not difficult to establish.
2. However, when the copy is not an identical or literal one, the test of infringement will be based on a two-prong test (*Francis Day and Hunter v Bron* (1963)).
3. It was held by the Court of Appeal in *Francis Day and Hunter v Bron* (1963) that in order to constitute copying, there must be:

**(a) a sufficient degree of objective similarity between the two works; and**
**(b) some casual connection between the original and the allegedly infringing work.**

4. Copying in relation to a literary, dramatic, musical or artistic work means reproducing the work in any material form, including storing the work in any medium by electronic means (s17(2)).

5. Copying in relation to an artistic work includes the making of a copy in three dimensions of a two-dimensional work and the making of a copy in two dimensions of a three-dimensional work (s17(3)).
6. Copying in relation to a film, television or broadcast or cable programme includes making a photograph of the whole or any substantial part of any image forming part of the film, broadcast or cable programme (s17(4)).
7. For typographical arrangement of a published edition, copying means making a facsimile copy of the arrangement (s17(5)).

### 12.2.2 Objective similarity and casual connection

1. There is no requirement that the works are identical in order to constitute infringement.
2. Where the whole work is not copied, the requirement is that a substantial part has been copied.
3. 'Substantial part' is subject to a qualitative test, not a quantitative one (*Ladbroke v William Hill* (1964)).
4. There should be a sufficient degree of similarity with the previous work, which the court identifies using an objective test (*Designers Guild Ltd v Russell Williams (Textiles) Ltd* (2001)).
5. Once sufficient similarity is established, it must also be shown that the infringing work must have originated in the plaintiff's.
6. Similarity devoid of a casual connection with the earlier work does not infringe.
7. The later work may qualify for independent copyright protection even though there is infringement of a substantial part of an earlier work.

### 12.2.3 Adaptations

1. The copyright owner of a literary, dramatic or musical work has the exclusive right to make an adaptation of the work (s16(1)(e) CDPA 1988).
2. 'Adaptation' in relation to a literary or dramatic work (see s21(3)(a)) means:
   (a) a translation of the work;
   (b) a version of a dramatic work in which it is converted into a non-dramatic form or vice versa;
   (c) a version of the work in which the story or the action is conveyed wholly or mainly by means of pictures in a form suitable for reproduction in a book, newspaper or journal.
3. 'Adaptation' in relation to a musical work means an arrangement or transcription of the work (s21(3)(b) CDPA 1988).
4. The rights of the copyright owner in the original work extend to the adaptations as well.
5. The adaptation must relate to a substantial part of the copyright work to infringe (*Sillitoe v McGraw-Hill Book Co (UK) Ltd* (1983)).

### 12.2.4 Computer programs

1. It is often difficult to establish substantiality and similarity for non-literal copying of computer programs.
2. This is because programs can be written in different computer languages which may eventually have very similar functions (*Ibcos Computers Ltd v Poole* (1994)).
3. In the United States, a three prong test of 'abstraction, filtration and comparison' is applied to determine non-literal infringement of computer programs (*Computer Associates International Inc v Altai Inc* (1992)).
4. First, the non-literal elements of the program's structures are separated by a process of abstraction, beginning from the

code until the end function of the program.

5. Second, the parts that are not entitled to copyright protection are filtered out, leaving a core of copyright protection.
6. Finally, similarities between the two programs are determined and if a substantial part of the later work forms part of the plaintiff's program that is protected by copyright, non-literal infringement can be established.
7. Some of the traditional principles applied to literary works cannot be applied as such to computer programs (*Cantor Fitzgerald International v Tradition (UK) Ltd* (2000)).
8. The practical test will be to determine whether the copied code represents a substantial part of the programmer's skill, which relates to the program's originality.

## 12.3 Authorising Infringement

1. To authorise another to do any of the restricted acts in a copyright work constitutes infringement (s16(2) CDPA 1988).

### 12.3.1 Linking

1. Hyperlinks are vital to the World Wide Web.
2. If hypertext links to copyright works are provided without the owner's permission, does that constitute infringement?
3. There is a delicate issue here of balancing the rights of copyright owners and at the same time not hindering the growth of the World Wide Web, as linking is crucial to the way the Internet works.
4. Providing a hyperlink to another website in itself does not infringe, unless the link itself is a copyright work.
5. There have been interesting issues raised in the cases of 'deep linking', where the link does not take the user to the home page of the website, but instead leads to one of the

subsidiary web pages within the site (*Shetland Times Ltd v Wills* (1996).

6. This could result in loss of revenue for the website as the user may skip the advertisements, or any other relevant information in the home page.

### 12.3.2 Framing

1. Framing raises issues for copyright law.
2. Frames work in such a manner that the content hosted in a different website might appear to be held in the linker's webpage itself.

## 12.4 SECONDARY INFRINGEMENT (ss22–26 CDPA 1988)

1. Secondary infringement usually involves commercial dealing of infringing copies, or providing the means for their manufacture.
2. It includes possessing, selling, exhibiting or distributing infringing copies, and importing infringing copies into the UK.
3. An infringing copy is a copy whose making constituted an infringement of the copyright in the work in question (s27(2) CDPA 1988).
4. The infringer must have knowledge, or at least have reason to believe that the copy is an infringing one.
5. Reason to believe means knowledge of the facts from which a reasonable man would arrive at the relevant belief, provided he had sufficient time to investigate the facts in order to acquire the reasonable belief (*LA Gear v Hi-Tec Sport* (1992); *Sillitoe v McGraw Hill Book Co (UK) Ltd* (1983)).
6. It is secondary infringement to make, import, possess in the course of business or to sell or hire any item that is designed or adapted for making copies of a copyright work, if the person believes or has reason to believe that the item will be

used in order to make infringing copies of that work (s24(1) CDPA 1988).

7. Where the copyright in a literary, dramatic or musical work is infringed by a performance at a place of public entertainment, any person who gave permission for that place to be used for the performance is also liable for the infringement unless when he gave permission he believed on reasonable grounds that the performance would not infringe copyright (s25(1) CDPA 1988).
8. In this case, the person who supplied the apparatus for infringing performance also is liable for the infringement if he knew or had reason to believe that the apparatus was likely to be used to infringe copyright (s26(2) CDPA 1988).
9. A copyright owner may be able to prevent parallel import of copies made outside the EEA, irrespective of whether they were made under license or not.
10. The copyright owner may have an interest in doing so especially if there is a price differential or the articles imported are of inferior quality.
11. To decide if the importation constitutes infringement, s27(3) CDPA 1988 stipulates a 'hypothetical manufacture' test.
12. If the goods were made in the UK, and not abroad, there is infringement if such a manufacture in the UK would have constituted infringement or the breach of a license.
13. The Copyright and Related Rights Regulations 2003 (CRRR 2003) have inserted certain criminal offences to the CDPA 1988 in order to check piracy of copyright works (ss107, 297 and 297A CDPA 1988).

## 12.5 Introduction to the Permitted Acts and Defences

### 12.5.1 Permissible acts and defences

1. There are certain acts that are permissible, which are expressly set out in the CDPA 1988 without which such acts

would normally be considered infringing. There are other defences which may run alongside these.

### 12.5.2 Fair dealing and additional defences

1. 'Fair dealing' is the most important of all permitted acts in relation to copyright.
2. The fair dealing defence is available for the following purposes:
   (i) research or private study;
   (ii) criticism or review;
   (iii) reporting current events.
3. Fair dealing defence is available only in relation to copyright and does not affect any other right or obligation restricting the doing of any of the specified acts, for example breach of confidence or a contract (s28(1) CDPA 1988).
4. Note that works may be independently inspired by the same source or constrained by the same functions that they will perform: *Francis Day & Hunter v Bron* (1963). Independent creation is a defence to copyright infringement
5. Note the public interest defence is relevant, as discussed at 10.4. Other defences such as acquiescence and implied licence may be pleaded, although these are not common. Acquiescence may occur if a right holder has known of infringement but has done nothing about it (*Farmers Build v Carier Bulk Handling Materials* (1999)). An argument for implied license may arise where practice suggests infringement should not occur, but this is often unsuccessful (*Banier v News Group* (1997); *Gabrin v Universal Music Operations Ltd* (2003)).
6. Note the issue of exhaustion of rights. After first sale, the right over distribution ceases. See e.g. *Egmont Films v Laserdisken* (1998). The right to control how the product is resold within an internal market is lost.

## 12.6 FAIR DEALING

### 12.6.1 Research and private study

1. Fair dealing with a literary, dramatic, musical or artistic work for the purposes of research or private study does not infringe any copyright in the work (s29(1) CDPA 1988).
2. In the case of a published edition, this applies to the typographical arrangement.
3. The fair dealing defence is not available for study or research undertaken for commercial purposes (s178 CDPA 1988 as amended by CRRR 2003).
4. Fair dealing for non-commercial research will not infringe provided it is accompanied by sufficient acknowledgment.
5. Although private study or research is not defined, case law suggests that the study must be for the person's own use (*Sillitoe v McGraw-Hill Book Co (UK) Ltd* (1983)).
6. Similarly, fair dealing for research or private study only covers the production of single copies. Multiple copies will infringe (s29(3) CDPA 1988).

### 12.6.2 Criticism, review and reporting

1. Fair dealing with a work for the purpose of criticism or review, of that or another work or of a performance of a work, does not infringe any copyright in the work provided that it is accompanied by sufficient acknowledgment and the work must have been made available to the public by an authorised act (s30(1) CDPA 1988).
2. Publication includes issuing copies to the public, making available by electronic retrieval systems, rental or lending of copies to the public, performance, exhibition, playing or showing, or communicating the work to the public.
3. Sufficient acknowledgment is defined as an acknowledgment identifying the work in question by its title or other description, and identifying the author. The exception to

this rule is if the work is unpublished or published anonymously and the author cannot be identified through a reasonable inquiry (s178(1) CDPA 1988).

4. This defence is available for multiple copies as well.
5. Fair dealing with a work other than a photograph for the purpose of reporting current events does not infringe provided that it is accompanied by a sufficient acknowledgment (s30(2) CDPA 1988).
6. No acknowledgment is required in connection with the reporting of current events by means of a sound recording, film, broadcast or cable programme (s30(3) CDPA 1988).

## 12.7 Incidental Inclusion of Copyright Material

### 12.7.1 Incidental inclusion

1. Copyright in a work is not infringed by its incidental inclusion in an artistic work, sound recording, film or broadcast (s31(1) CDPA 1988).
2. Nor does it infringe to issue copies to the public, or the playing, showing or broadcasting of such works (s31(2) CDPA 1988).
3. However, a musical work, words spoken or sung with music, or so much of a sound recording or broadcast as includes a musical work or such words, shall not be regarded as incidentally included in another work if it is deliberately included (s31(3) CDPA 1988).

### 12.7.2 Definition of incidental

1. 'Incidental' is not defined.
2. However, case law accords its ordinary meaning of 'casual', 'unintentional' or 'non-deliberate' (*IPC Magazines Ltd v MGN Ltd* (1998)), although 'incidental' is not confined to these meanings alone (*Football Association Premier League Ltd v Panini UK Ltd* (2003)).

## 12.8 Instruction or Examination

1. If the copying of a literary, dramatic, musical or artistic work is done in the course of instruction or of preparation for instruction it does not infringe, provided (s32(1) CDPA 1988):
   (a) it is done by a person giving or receiving instruction; and
   (b) is not by means of a reprographic process.
2. Reprographic process is defined as a process for making facsimile copies or involving the use of an appliance for making multiple copies including photocopying, facsimile machines and scanners.
3. Similarly, copyright in a sound recording, film or broadcast is not infringed by its being copied by making a film or film soundtrack in the course of instruction, or of preparation for instruction, in the making of films or film soundtracks, provided the copying is done by a person giving or receiving instruction (s32(2) CDPA 1988).
4. There is no infringement for anything done for the purposes of an examination, including setting the questions, communicating the questions to the candidates or answering questions.
5. Anthologies from a published literary and dramatic work can be included in collections of works intended for use in educational establishments, subject to conditions (s33 CDPA 1988).
6. For example, the inclusion of more than two excerpts from copyright works by the same author in collections published by the same publisher over any period of five years is not authorised by the above provision.

## 12.9 Public Administration

1. Anything done for the purposes of judicial proceedings will not be copyright infringement (s45 CDPA 1988).

2. There is no requirement of fair dealing for copying made for the purpose of judicial proceedings.
3. There is no restriction on making multiple copies either.
4. It is also permitted to copy with the authority of the appropriate person of any material that is open to inspection by statute provided it is not intended to issue those copies to the public (s47 CDPA 1988).
5. However, it is permitted to issue copies to the public as long as it is intended purely for the purpose of facilitating the right of public inspection.

## 12.10 Home Copying

1. Home copying for various purposes including entertainment and private study raise a number of interesting issues for copyright law.
2. Home recording or downloading of sound recordings, films and broadcasts including any underlying works constitutes infringement.
3. However, recording a radio or television broadcast in domestic premises for private and domestic use does not infringe copyright in the broadcast or rights in performances, subject to the condition below (s70(1) CDPA 1988).
4. This is subject to a condition that the recording must be made only for viewing or listening to at a more convenient time, usually called 'time-shifting'.

## 12.11 Performance in an Educational Establishment

1. The performance of a literary, dramatic or musical work before an audience consisting of teachers and pupils at an educational establishment does not infringe (s34(1) CDPA 1988).
2. This is subject to the provision that the performance was made either:

(a) by a teacher or pupil in the course of the activities of the establishment, or
(b) at the establishment by any person for the purposes of instruction.

3. To play or show a sound recording, film or broadcast before such an audience at an educational establishment does not constitute a playing or showing of the work in public for the purposes of copyright infringement (s34(2) CDPA 1988).
4. Parents of a pupil are not included as part for the establishment for this defence.

## 12.12 Computer Programs

1. The Software Directive was incorporated into the CDPA 1988 through the Copyright (Computer Programs) Regulations 1992 which provided special provisions for the lawful use of computer programs.
2. Lawful use means the user should be licensed to use the program.
3. It is permitted to make necessary back-up copies of a program by lawful users (s50A CDPA 1988).
4. The making of back-up copies cannot be excluded by contract.
5. Lawful users of a program are entitled to observe, study or test the functioning of a program to determine or analyse the ideas and principles underlying any element of it, when loading, displaying, running, transmitting or storing it.
6. The provision for making back-up copies does not apply to copy-protected computer games CDs (*Sony Computer Entertainment v Ball* (2004)).

## 12.13 The Internet

1. The use of the Internet involves the making of temporary copies, commonly known as caching.
2. Strictly speaking, these transient copies should infringe as reproduction applies to storage by electronic means as well

as copies transient or incidental to some other use of the work (s17(2) CDPA 1988).

3. The CRRR 2003 has added new defences to address this issue (s28A CDPA 1988).
4. Therefore, it does not infringe copyright, except in a computer program or database, to make temporary copies which are:
   (a) transient or incidental;
   (b) an essential and integral part of a technological process;
   (c) the copies are made exclusively for the purpose of enabling the transmission of the work in a network between third parties by an intermediary, or a lawful use of the work;
   (d) have no economic significance in itself.

# INDEX

## Key Cases

*Series Editors: Jacqueline Martin and Chris Turner*

**Key Cases** has been specifically written for students studying law. It is the essential revision tool to be used on its own or with the partner **Key Facts** title in order to ensure a thorough knowledge of core cases for any given law topic.

Understanding essential and leading cases fully is a vital part of the study of law – the clear format, style and explanations of **Key Cases** will ensure you have this understanding.

The series is written and edited by an expert team of authors whose experience means they know exactly what is required in a revision aid. They include lecturers and barristers who have brought their expertise and knowledge to the series to make it user-friendly and accessible.

Key features include:

- All essential and leading cases explained
- User-friendly layout and style
- Cases broken down into key components by use of clear symbol system
- Pocket-sized and easily portable
- Highly-regarded authors and editors

# Unlocking the Law

*Series Editors: Jacqueline Martin and Chris Turner*

**Unlocking the Law** is a series of textbooks with a unique approach to undergraduate study of law, designed specifically so that the subject matter is readable and that students are not overwhelmed with page after page of continuous prose.

The text of each title is broken up with features and activities that have been written to ensure that students are pointed in the right direction when it comes to understanding the purpose of different areas within the course. All titles in the series follow the same format and include the same features so that students can move easily from one law subject to another.

The series covers all the core subjects required by the Bar Council and the Law Society for entry onto professional qualifications and will expand to include titles on option areas.

**Unlocking the Law** includes the following titles:

| | | |
|---|---|---|
| Unlocking Constitutional & Administrative Law | 978 0 340 81606 6 | **NEW** |
| Unlocking Contract Law 2nd edition | 978 0 340 94196 6 | **NEW** |
| Unlocking Criminal Law 2nd edition | 978 0 340 94199 7 | **NEW** |
| Unlocking The English Legal System | 978 0 340 88693 9 | |
| Unlocking EU Law | 978 0 340 88759 2 | |
| Unlocking Land Law 2nd edition | 978 0 340 94198 0 | **NEW** |
| Unlocking Legal Learning | 978 0 340 88761 5 | |
| Unlocking Torts 2nd edition | 978 0 340 94197 3 | **NEW** |
| Unlocking Trusts | 978 0 340 88694 6 | |